how to
modernize a
BASEMENT

Family Room • Rental Apartment

Donald R. Brann

ELEVENTH PRINTING — 1978
REVISED EDITION

Published by
DIRECTIONS SIMPLIFIED, INC.

Division of
EASI-BILD PATTERN CO., INC.
Briarcliff Manor, NY 10510

Library of Congress Card No. 66-22941

FIRST PRINTING
© 1966

REVISED EDITIONS
1967,1968,1969,1970,
1972,1973,1974,1976
1978

NOTE
Due to the variance in quality and availability of many materials and products, always follow directions a manufacturer and/or retailer offers. Unless products are used exactly as the manufacturer specifies, its warranty can be voided. While the author mentions certain products by trade name, no endorsement or end use guarantee is implied. In every case the author suggests end uses as specified by the manufacturer prior to publication.

Since manufacturers frequently change ingredients or formula and/or introduce new and improved products, or fail to distribute in certain areas, trade names are mentioned to help the reader zero in on products of comparable quality and end use.   The Publisher

TAKE A DEEP BREATH

We live in a strange and wondrous age. One in which science solves many of mankind's most complex problems, while millions of hardworking men and women can't obtain the help they desperately need to solve everyday problems. Baffled by tensions and fears they can't handle, thousands of minds and marriages break every year. Millions fail to breathe normally.

If you find yourself breathing less and worrying more, take a deep breath, start moving in a new direction. Remember, deep breathing accentuates the positive. Focus your mind on a spare time activity that requires physical and mental effort. Plunge into a new sphere of activity.

Doing something today, you didn't believe yourself capable of doing yesterday, helps reorient your thinking. The physical work stimulates the blood stream, helps tone muscles, while the concentration provides escape from other problems. Since you only drive one nail or saw one board at a time, you will be agreeably surprised to see how quickly you can synchronize proper breathing with physical effort.

Solving problems, regardless of whether they are mental, physical or financial, like deep breathing, is the key to living. We begin to die long before we have learned to live if we allow fear to curtail action. Invest every spare hour doing physical work and see how quickly you feel better, how easily you learn to breathe properly, how much more living you get out of life.

Don R. Brann

TABLE OF CONTENTS

TIME — YOUR MOST PRECIOUS POSSESSION

Years ago, when the original edition of this book went on sale, life was lived under far different circumstances. A basement was most often a catch all, housing costs were 300% less than today, folks could walk safely on city streets after dark. As the cost per square foot of housing increased, basements became family rooms. Now they are being used as income producers, hungrily sought after by singles desirous of living in the comparative safety of the suburbs.

Homeowners who need an apartment with a separate entry for an aged parent, find a modernized basement an economical housing solution. While local codes frown on two family occupancy in areas zoned for single family dwellings, this conversion is usually acceptable. Later on, the apartment can become an important source of income. It's amazing how many "kissin' cousins" surface when a singles apartment is available in a safe neighborhood.

This book assumes the reader has never modernized a basement and explains every step. It tells what materials to buy, when and where each is used. Whether you do part, all or none of the work, substantial savings will be effected when you purchase materials. Even more will be saved when you transform spare time into building labor. Improving your home provides one of the soundest investments you can make. Your spare time can add thousands of dollars to its value.

The first step is to read through this book completely. Note each illustration when mentioned. If any step is not entirely clear, ask your building material dealer to explain.

Next make a list of end uses. Do you need a laundry, sewing or recreation room, an extra bedroom, workshop, more storage space? Will the basement be transformed into an apartment for an aged parent? Do you need extra income to meet mortgage payments and taxes? Place the most important reasons on top of your list. Next draw a plan. Use the grid on page 98. Consider each box one foot. Does space allocated for one end use allow sufficient room to satisfy other needs.

Modernizing a basement follows this general procedure:
1. Install outside entry door and stairs.
2. Repair cracks in floor and walls.
3. Remove a window or cut opening for air conditioner.
4. Waterproof walls.
5. Level floor with underlayment.
6. Build partitions.
7. Rough in wiring, plumbing and heating.
8. Panel walls.
9. Install fluorescent lighting, acoustic ceiling.
10. Build base and wall cabinets.
11. Lay asphalt, vinyl or quarry tile flooring.
12. Set plumbing fixtures.
13. Hang doors.
14. Apply trim.

If you need a laundry, bathroom or kitchen, it's more economical to locate it adjacent to waste, vent and water lines. If gas appliances are to be installed, these require an outside vent. The space required for a laundry room depends on equipment selected, plus sufficient shelving to accommodate detergents, bleaches, spot removers, etc.; a counter for sorting clothes, space to hang or stack finished work. The door to this room should be 2'8" or larger.

If the basement floor is lower than your sewer line, make certain the washing machine pump has sufficient power to lift water to height required. If necessary, an auxiliary pump can be installed. This isn't a difficult or costly problem, so don't let anyone con you into thinking it's a big deal. In many cases, if you build a platform, using 2 x 4, 2 x 6 or 2 x 8's on edge, plus ¾" plyscord, you raise the fixture just enough so its pump works efficiently.

Once upon a time, living in a basement was considered equal in status to an attic bedroom. Nowadays, thanks to air conditioning, people consider any air conditioned room desirable, regardless of location. If your plan calls for a downstairs bedroom or living room, locate it adjacent to a window or a window can be removed and an air conditioning unit installed. If no cellar window is convenient, cut an opening to size required.

The ideal location for a recreation room is off the stairway. Space below stairs can be enclosed for storage, TV niche, etc.

If a basement workshop is on your list, locate it adjacent to an outside door. This simplifies handling lumber, panels of plywood, etc.

Dividing a basement to obtain rooms needed requires extra lighting, additional wall outlets and sometimes more housepower. Ask the utility company to check capacity of present service line. Explain what you plan, and they can install a heavier service line if same is needed. Book #694 Electrical Repairs Simplified provides considerable help.

ENTRY THROUGH FOUNDATION*

Locate outside entry where it is readily accessible, and where it doesn't interfere with future plans for a garage, patio, etc. Since you may want to bring in bulky pieces, be sure entry door and doors in basement partitions are aligned. Install a 3'0" x 6'8" or 2'8" x 6'8" basement door, nothing smaller.

Those creating a rental basement apartment can greatly enhance its potential by building a walk through greenhouse entry, Illus. 92. The overall size of footing and foundation is shown in Illus. 2A. Step-by-step directions for building the greenhouse are detailed in Book #611 How to Build a Walk-In and Window Greenhouse.

Installation of a grade level entry with inside stairs, Illus. 94, enhances an income producing apartment. Locate entry so it insures privacy for tenant and landlord and is readily accessible to street or driveway.

Using a level and chalk, draw lines on wall, Illus. 1, to indicate rough opening. If site selected contains a window, same can be removed. Do not cut an opening closer than 2'10" from a window. If a prefabricated basement enclosure is to be removed and a walk-in greenhouse constructed, lay foundation to size shown, Illus. 2A.

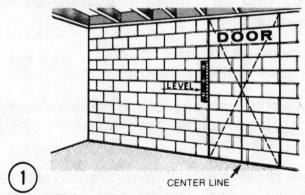

CENTER LINE

Foundation dimensions shown in Illus. 2 will accommodate a prefabricated steel basement enclosure, complete with torsion bar doors. This enclosure is only recommended when basement is used for storage.

*Installation of a grade level entry door begins on page 69.

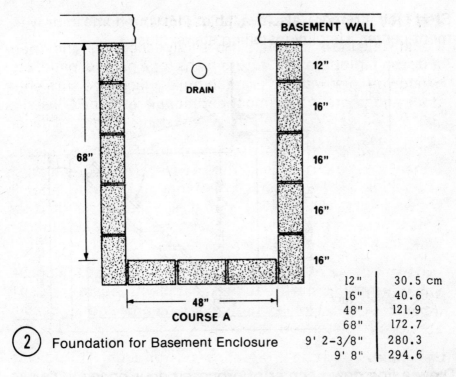

12"	30.5 cm
16"	40.6
48"	121.9
68"	172.7
9' 2-3/8"	280.3
9' 8"	294.6

(2) Foundation for Basement Enclosure

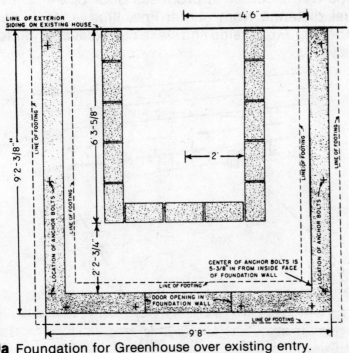

(2)a Foundation for Greenhouse over existing entry.

11

Steel stair stringers, also available from your home improvement center, simplify installing stairs, Illus. 3.

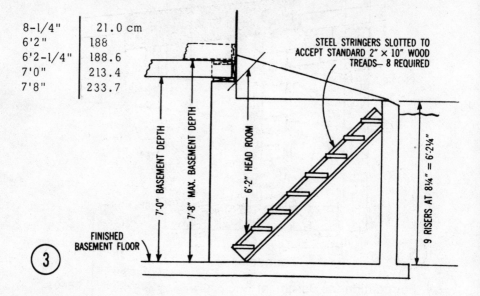

8-1/4"	21.0 cm
6'2"	188
6'2-1/4"	188.6
7'0"	213.4
7'8"	233.7

STEEL STRINGERS SLOTTED TO ACCEPT STANDARD 2" × 10" WOOD TREADS— 8 REQUIRED

7'-0" BASEMENT DEPTH

7'-8" MAX. BASEMENT DEPTH

6'-2" HEAD ROOM

9 RISERS AT 8¼" = 6'-2¼"

FINISHED BASEMENT FLOOR

③

Draw a line down center of proposed door opening. Draw lines equal distance from center line, Illus. 1, to indicate width of opening. Go outside and stake out excavation, Illus. 4.

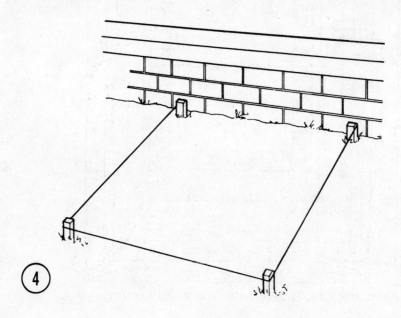

④

⑤

Excavate to depth of house footing, Illus. 5.

Level bottom of excavated area, Illus. 6.

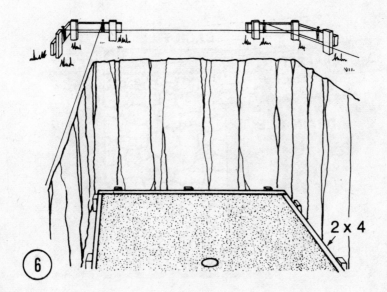

2 x 4

⑥

Locate a drain where it can carry water to tile along house footings, Illus. 7, or to a dry well.

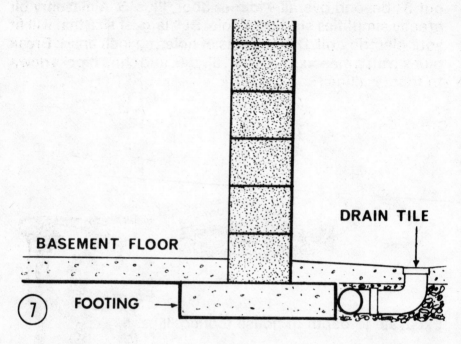

DRAIN TILE

BASEMENT FLOOR

⑦ **FOOTING** →

If existing drain is too high, run tile to a dry well, Illus. 8.

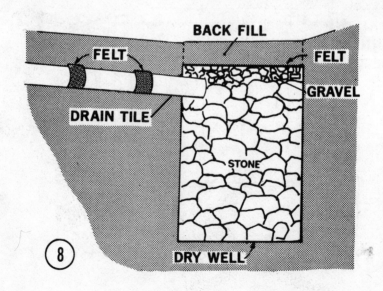

BACK FILL

FELT

FELT

GRAVEL

DRAIN TILE

STONE

⑧

DRY WELL

Opening for door can be made with a cold chisel and hammer. Start at center, Illus. 1, and work out. Chip blocks out 3″ beyond overall width of door, Illus. 5. A masonry bit greatly simplifies starting a hole. Buy largest size that will fit your electric drill. Drill a series of holes an inch apart. Break block with a mason's hammer, Illus. 9, and chop blocks down to footing, Illus. 5.

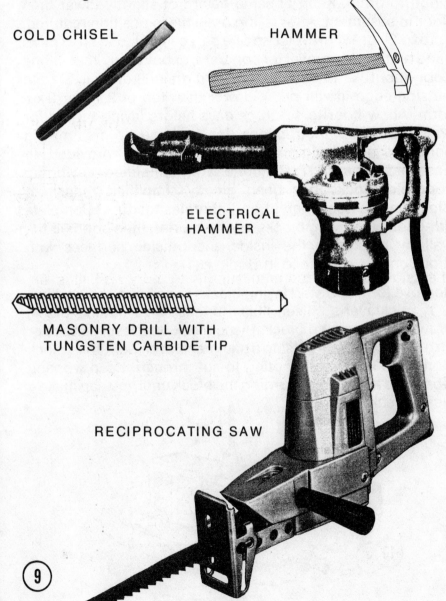

COLD CHISEL

HAMMER

ELECTRICAL
HAMMER

MASONRY DRILL WITH
TUNGSTEN CARBIDE TIP

RECIPROCATING SAW

⑨

If basement is poured concrete, rent an electric hammer with a slotting tool recommended by dealer. Also rent a heavy duty reciprocating saw and metal cutting blade to cut through the steel reinforcing rods or wire usually imbedded in a poured concrete wall.

Build forms for floor, Illus. 6, using 2 x 4 or 2 x 6. Floor should slope to drain. Keep at same height or slightly lower than floor in basement. After laying drain tile in position required, spread 2" of ¾" gravel. Use one part cement to 2½ to 3 parts sand and 5 parts gravel for concrete, or buy ready-mix. Slope floor about ⅛" to each foot toward drain. If drain is 2' from outside edge, it will be ¼" lower than top of 2 x 4 or 2 x 6 form. Allow floor to set three days before laying blocks for walls. Detailed instructions for building forms, mixing concrete and laying concrete blocks are provided in Easi-Bild Book #617, Concrete Work Simplified. Laying up concrete blocks has been greatly simplified thanks to BlocBond, a new cement and fiberglas mixture. Complete directions for laying blocks dry, no mortar, then bonding the wall by plastering the inside and outside surfaces with BlocBond, is explained in Book #617.

Remove form and start laying blocks in position shown, Illus. 2. A bricklayer's chisel, Illus. 10, simplifies cutting block. Draw line all around block. Place block on a level surface or on a flat bag of sand. Using a hammer and chisel, strike block along line before attempting to cut through. Keep working along line as you keep turning the block until you can make a clean break.

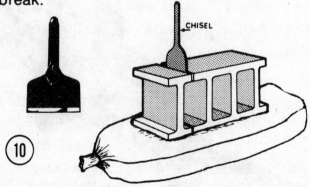

CHISEL

10

Stagger joints on each course as indicated in Illus. 2, 11. Lay course A, then B, then A, etc., Illus. 13.

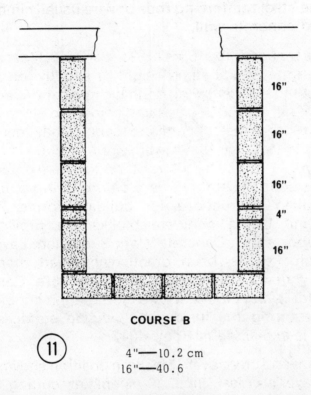

COURSE B

⑪   4"——10.2 cm
       16"——40.6

For a metal enclosure, build blocks up to one course above grade or to height enclosure directions suggest. For a greenhouse, lay three courses of block above grade. Most steel enclosures require 72" — 9 courses of 8" blocks, plus a 2¼" cap.

Fill half of core in top course with crushed balls of newspaper so you can pour concrete in core.

Build door frame, Illus. 12. Cut 2 x 10 to width of block and to length door requires. Drive 8 penny common nails into frame, Illus. 14. These anchor frame to concrete. Set in place, check with level and brace in position.

If two floor joists happen to be nailed together above area cut for door opening, use a double header over door.

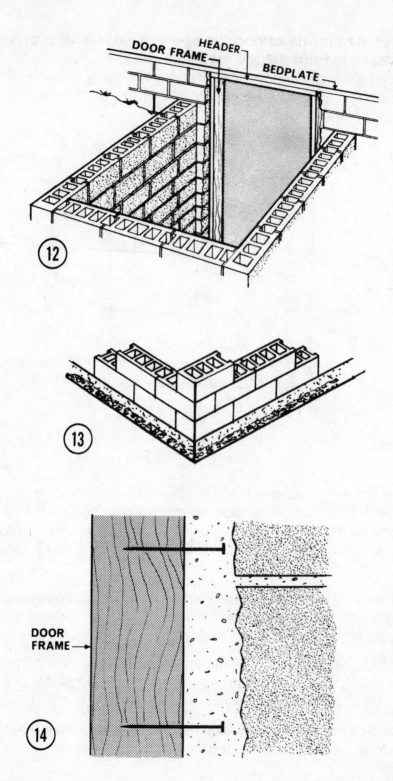

Nail 1 x 6 to inside of door frame as a temporary form. Nail braces, inside and out, to hold frame against block wall, Illus. 15. Nail through header to bedplate. If header doesn't butt against bedplate, cut 2 x 4 studs to length required and nail to header and bedplate.

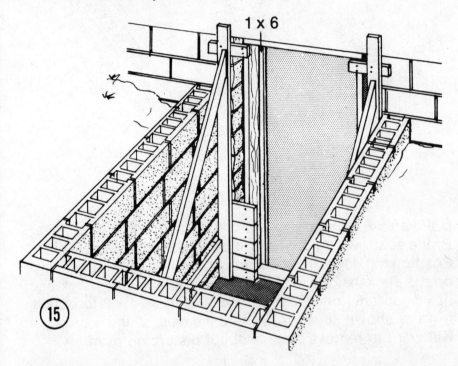

1 x 6

(15)

Start at bottom, hose footing and edge of block. Paint wet edge with a mushy mix of one part cement, two parts sand. Nail one, two or three short lengths of 1 x 6 to edge of door frame, brace other end against block, Illus. 15. Fill space with a 1:2:3* mix of concrete. Tap boards to settle concrete. Work concrete down with a stick to fill all pockets. Add more boards as you work your way up. Use a stiff, fairly dry mixture of concrete at top. When concrete has hardened sufficiently remove forms and smooth surface using a steel float.

Cover door opening with polyethylene and/or a panel of plywood. Don't nail plywood. Allow concrete to set three days to a week before installing a door. Use three 3½ x 3½" hinges.

*One part cement, two parts sand, three parts gravel.

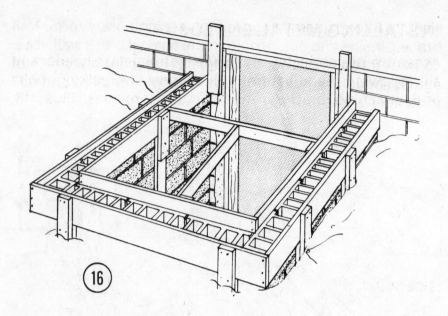

(16)

Build a 1 x 6 form for cap, Illus. 16. Temporarily nail to stakes. Brace as shown. Allow 1 x 6 to project about 4" above block. Position top edge of outside form board ¾" lower than inside board. Tack inside form to 1 x 2 cross ties. Keep 1 x 2 clear of hex head anchor fasteners, Illus. 18. Tack 1 x 2 to outside form as shown, Illus. 17. Don't drive nails all the way as you will want to remove these without disturbing form.

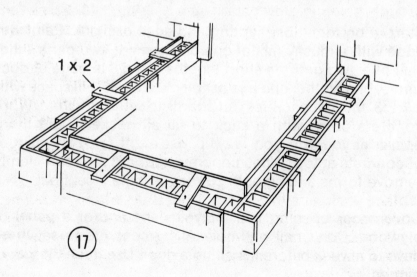

1 x 2

(17)

INSTALLING METAL ENCLOSURE

Assemble prefabricated enclosure side panels to header and sill following manufacturer's directions. Use calking, bolts and attaching brackets manufacturer provides, Illus. 18.

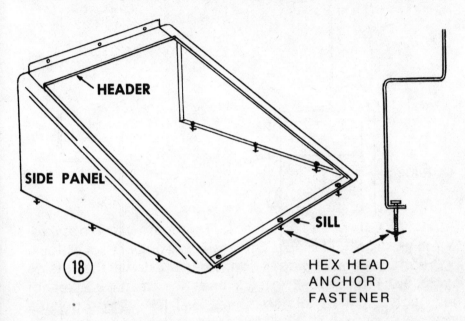

HEADER

SIDE PANEL

SILL

(18)

HEX HEAD
ANCHOR
FASTENER

Place slotted hex head screws, supplied by manufacturer, through holes in side panels and sill, Illus. 18. Screw on spring clip two or three threads. Place assembled enclosure in position on 1 x 2's, Illus. 19. Check with level. Draw outline of enclosure where it butts against house siding. Remove enclosure. With an electric hand saw, set to saw only through exterior siding, clapboard or shingle, saw siding within drawn area. Don't cut through roofing felt or sub-sheathing.

Install flashing and apply calking following direction provided by manufacturer of enclosure.

Replace enclosure in position and fasten header to house. Install doors following manufacturer's directions. Test open doors to make certain they work freely and set square in frame. If necessary, shim with pieces of shingle to hold frame square and level.

21

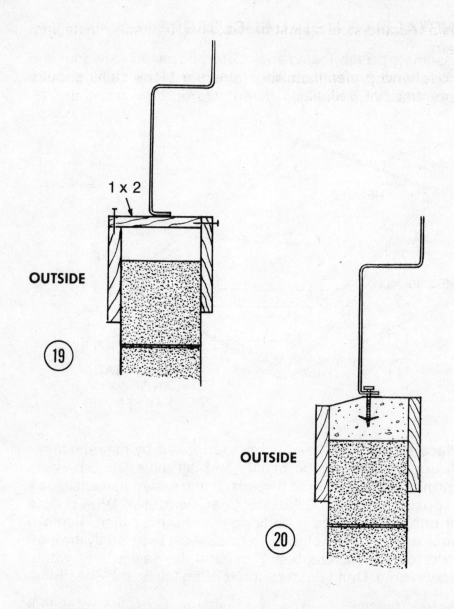

1 x 2

OUTSIDE

⑲

OUTSIDE

⑳

With anchor fasteners projecting below side panels and sills, Illus. 20, pour concrete into form and cores in block. Use one part cement to three parts sand. Slope cap as shown. When concrete begins to set, remove 1 x 2's and fill void with concrete. Allow concrete cap to set three days before removing form or operating doors. If you note any hairline cracks, use an acrylic latex sealant.

Prefabricated steel stair stringers, Illus. 3, simplify installing stairs.

Those who prefer installing concrete block steps should slope back of well, Illus. 21.

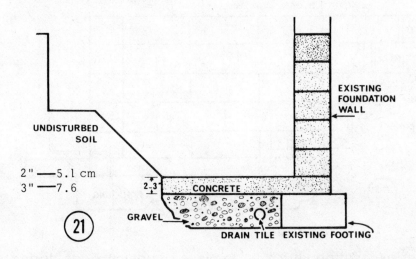

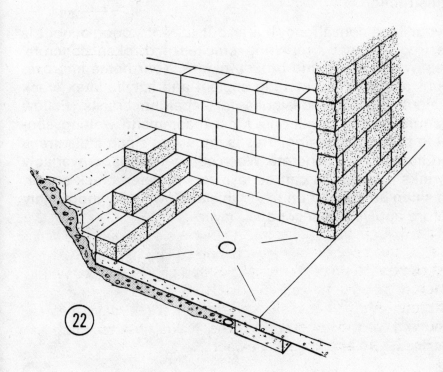

Cover undisturbed soil with 2" of gravel, Illus. 22. Set blocks in a thick bed of mortar. Allow each step to overlap block below 1", Illus. 22, 23.

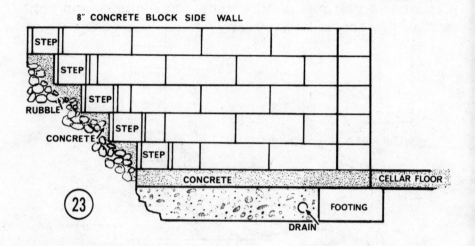

8" CONCRETE BLOCK SIDE WALL

Cover excavation with a large piece of polyethylene during construction.

If your basement already has an outside entry door, or none is desired, begin by repairing cracked or broken concrete. Remove all loose and broken pieces. Your home improvement dealer sells patching cement and acrylic latex crack sealants specially designed for repairing cracks. Follow manufacturer's directions. Most recommend wetting concrete prior to patching. This is important since moisture is required to cure concrete. When concrete dries, it invariably shrinks. Low spots can be leveled with latex crack sealer. This can be applied up to ¼" thick. Allow to dry thoroughly before applying a second ¼" layer.

TUCK-POINTING CONCRETE BLOCK

If basement wal contains joints that need to be refilled, clean out particles and wet joint. With float and small trowel, Illus. 24, push mortar into joint. Finish with jointer, Illus. 25. Use prepared mortar mix. Where joints show cracks and tight mortar, use acrylic latex sealer.

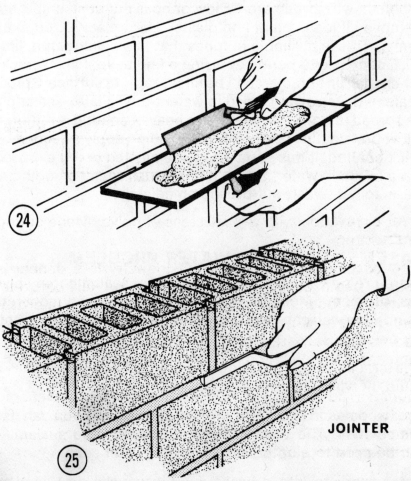

JOINTER

After making repairs to floors and walls, apply waterproofing following manufacturer's directions. Next show your basement plan to a plumber. He can tell you when he will want to rough in supply, drainage and vent lines. If partitioning in basement necessitates installation of extra radiators, now is the time to rough them in.

BASEMENT WITH A MOISTURE PROBLEM

This can be caused by water seeping down outside foundation wall or from pressure building up below floor. If water collects in one spot, you can frequently correct it by installing a sump pump. Note directions on page 30.

Where fine cracks, or particles of mortar indicate a moisture problem, wire brush area. Blow or hose out dust, chips, etc. Remove all loose paint and plaster. Use an acrylic concrete sealer. This is available in tubes that fit a calking gun, Illus. 40. Cut nozzle to permit applying a find bead. Fill all cracks. Where hairline cracks can't be filled, apply to surface. Spread sealer with a trowel dipped in water. Acrylic latex sealer can be spread up to ¼" thick. When a heavier coating is required, allow first coating to dry thoroughly then apply a second ¼" thick coating. If this surface is to be painted or left exposed, dip a brush in water. Shake it out. Brush sealer smooth and allow to set. Wash out brush immediately.

BASEMENTS WITH A WATER PROBLEM

There are now several different types of sealants that solve this problem. Moisture in a block or poured concrete foundation wall can frequently be remedied with waterproofing paint.

Fine cracks in mortar joints should be filled with either a liquid, acrylic latex sealant or epoxy.

Epoxy comes in two parts. Mix only as much as you can use immediately. The third sealant — called a plug sealant — can be used to plug cracks even with water seeping in.

Water seepage into a basement can usually be traced to concealed, or exposed cracks in mortar joints, in cracked blocks, or from pressure building up alongside, or under basement floor. Two of the most common causes are:

1. A poorly installed leader carrying rain water from gutters. If leader is clogged, a joint loose, or leader discharges too

close to foundation wall, it creates problems that can easily be rectified.

2. Hard to find, hairline cracks in mortar joints can frequently be located when you apply sufficient water at grade level.

Check each leader to make certain it drains away from foundation to either a run-off, or to a dry well. If you build a dry well, do so far enough and at a point lower than foundation so surrounding area can absorb run-off.

Seepage through cracks in mortar joints can be sealed in several different ways. If crack starts near grade level, Illus. 26, dig a trench with bottom of trench level with crack. Cover side, but not bottom of trench with polyethylene.* Soak trench with water so it filters into and soaks crack. Next pour in Hydro Stop or equal ready to use liquid sealant. Pour sealant into trench and it will seep into and fill crack. There are many different types of liquid sealants available so be sure to follow manufacturer's directions.

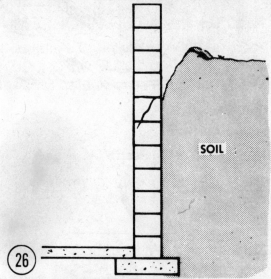

SOIL

26

Keep pouring sealant into trench until foundation refuses to absorb it. Wait awhile, then apply a fine mist of water and flush any sealant remaining in trench. Some of this will be absorbed by foundation.

*Polyethylene wrappers from your dry cleaner can be used.

Some hairline cracks frequently require a second application. Apply same 24 hours later. Again, wet trench with water to soak crack before applying second application.

If a crack starts below grade, where it's concealed on the outside by a concrete walk, but shows up inside basement, you can waterproof two ways. Using a carbide tipped masonry bit, rout out mortar on inside at least ½ to ¾" deep where crack appears. If you don't have an electric drill, use a can opener to make a ½ to ¾" deep V groove in crack. Remove all loose particles. Apply latex or epoxy sealant, Illus. 27. Since an epoxy sets up fast, use within time manufacturer specifies.

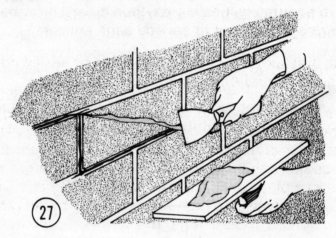

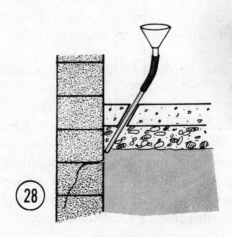

Allow sealant to set exact time manufacturer specifies then give the area a hosing. If water continues to appear, locate exact position of crack on inside by measuring over to a window or door, and from top of foundation down. Go outside. If a concrete walk covers area, drill a ½" or larger hole through concrete, Illus. 28, then drive a rod down to a depth just above crack. Remove rod and carefully insert a piece of copper tubing. Fasten a piece of rubber hose and funnel to top end. Fill funnel with water. When crack is saturated, pour in liquid sealant.

If you have a long crack, or if a portion of the foundation wall is allowing water to enter at several different levels, draw a chart to accurately locate area, then drive a crow bar or iron rod to depth required to service each course.

Cracks that take in a lot of water should be sealed inside with latex sealant, and on outside with liquid sealer.

Cracks that appear in a poured concrete wall inside basement can be handled in this manner. Drill a ½" or larger hole at top of crack. Drill hole at a slight downward angle to a distance halfway through wall. Use a ½" or larger masonry bit. Insert a piece of ½" copper tubing of sufficient length to penetrate halfway into foundation and still project at least 2" from wall. Use rubber tube and funnel. Apply water, then sealant as described above. Keep pouring until it won't take any more. Wait 15 to 20 minutes and try again. If it still won't take more, remove pipe and seal hole with latex sealant. This repair doesn't work in concrete block walls.

If a basement wall or floor is subjected to fairly strong water pressure, use a fast setting plug sealant.*This comes in a powder and is mixed with water. It dries to a hard metallic finish in minutes. Plug sealants can also be used to anchor bolts or fasteners in concrete. Only mix as much as you need. Don't mix a new batch with any part of a previous batch. Most patching plug sealants are applied to a thoroughly soaked surface. Use a short bladed putty knife. Work the sealant in fast, deep and smooth, as quickly as possible.

*WATERPLUG - Use exactly as manufacturer specifies.

SUMP PUMP INSTALLATION

Note Illus. 29.

Rent an electric hammer or equal type of tool to break through concrete. Since you can break through in very little time, rent the tool on an hourly rate. Cut a hole in floor to size and depth recommended by sump pump manufacturer, but don't purchase pump until you have made this test. Dig hole to depth pump requires, then fill bottom with 3 to 4" of ¾" gravel. place a 12 to 18" diameter drain tile vertically in position. Test hole to see if it collects water.

Drain tiles designed for sump pump installation are perforated to permit seepage. Backfill around tile with 3 to 4" of crushed stone. If you can't buy a cap for the drain tile, make one using two pieces of ¾" exterior grade plywood. Cut to diameter required. Glue together using waterproof glue.

Position top edge of tile flush or a hair less than level of floor.

Cut a slot in cap for discharge pipe and wire cable. Drill additional ½ or ¾" holes in cap to vent pump. Paint cap with waterproof sealant.

Prior to buying and installing a pump, buy an inexpensive bilge pump from a marine supply store. Use this to empty water from drain tile. If the tile catches seepage, buy pump that accommodates flow of water. Follow manufacturer's directions and run discharge pipe from pump to a dry well. Since you will have to go through basement wall to discharge water to a dry well, cut through foundation at highest possible point.

If your basement is damp, install a humidifier. Select size with sufficient capacity to handle overall cubage of basement.

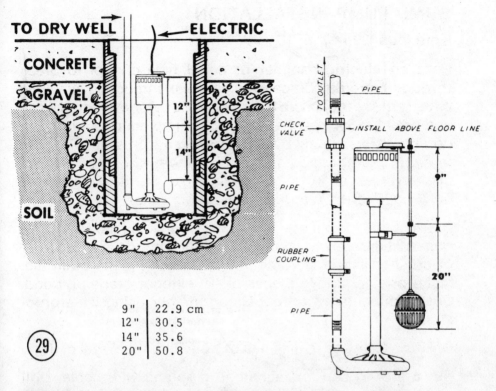

TO DRY WELL — ELECTRIC
CONCRETE
GRAVEL
SOIL
12"
14"

TO OUTLET
PIPE
CHECK VALVE
PIPE
RUBBER COUPLING
PIPE
INSTALL ABOVE FLOOR LINE
9"
20"

9"	22.9 cm
12"	30.5
14"	35.6
20"	50.8

(29)

ROUGH IN SUPPLY AND DRAINAGE LINES

Where a basement is being transformed into an apartment, a separate bathroom and kitchen are essential. Book #682 How to Install an Extra Bathroom and #658 How to Build Kitchen Cabinets provide much helpful information.

Where the sewer or septic tank waste line is lower than basement floor, drainage lines can be connected with no problem.

Where sewer line is floor level, you can frequently install a complete bathroom and kitchen by positioning same over 2 x 6 or 2 x 8 floor joists, Illus. 29A. Cover joists with ¾" exterior grade plywood.

Where a sewer line is above floor level, a jet-powered john, Illus. 29B, can be installed. This toilet flushes waste up to 10' height. Your plumber can install a booster pump that will accommodate a kitchen sink, lavatory and bathtub.

31

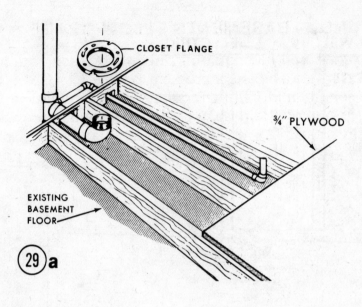

CLOSET FLANGE

¾″ PLYWOOD

EXISTING BASEMENT FLOOR

29 a

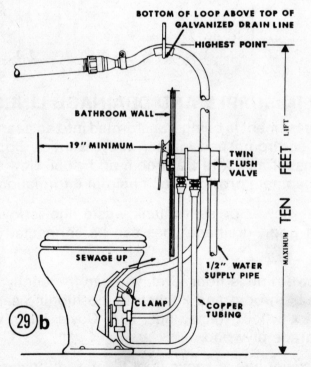

BOTTOM OF LOOP ABOVE TOP OF GALVANIZED DRAIN LINE

HIGHEST POINT

BATHROOM WALL

19″ MINIMUM

TEN FEET LIFT

MAXIMUM

TWIN FLUSH VALVE

SEWAGE UP

1/2″ WATER SUPPLY PIPE

CLAMP

COPPER TUBING

29 b

Always position a jet-powered toilet as close to sewer line as possible.

A bathroom installation must meet local code requirements.

32

FURRING — BASEMENTS BELOW GRADE

Rather than nail furring strips directly to a concrete block wall and create a moisture problem, build a 2 x 4 frame, Illus. 30, to length and height required. Always measure from highest point on floor. Cut a stud to height you think will tip up. Nail blocks of 2 x 4 to represent a shoe and plate. Test it in position all along wall. To play safe, cut studs to length that permits raising with wedges.

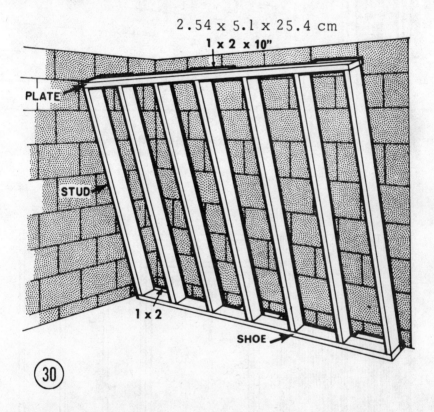

2.54 x 5.1 x 25.4 cm
1 x 2 x 10"

PLATE

STUD

1 x 2

SHOE

30

Nail shoe and plate to studs with 16 penny nails. Where there's any moisture problem, staple aluminum building paper to back of frame. Nail 4 to 6" pieces of 1 x 2 to shoe and plate every four feet to fur frame out from wall.

Place frame in position, check with level to make certain it's plumb, then wedge frame against ceiling joists by driving wood shingle or wedges cut to size required under shoe.

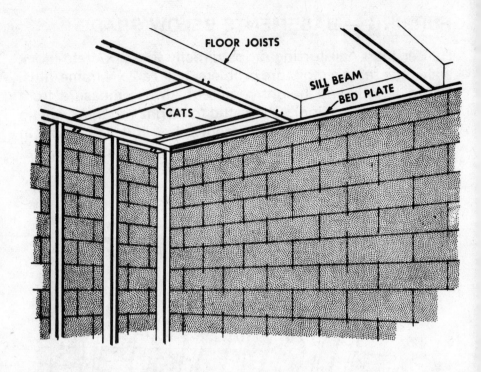

FLOOR JOISTS

SILL BEAM

BED PLATE

CATS

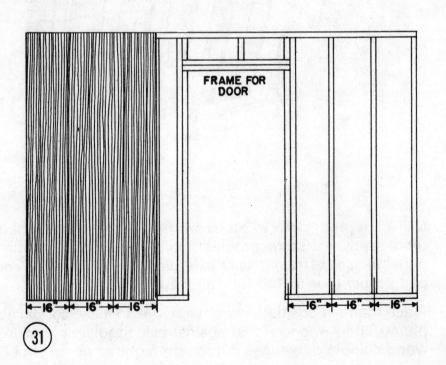

FRAME FOR DOOR

|← 16" →|← 16" →|← 16" →|

|← 16" →|← 16" →|← 16" →|

(31)

Nail plate to ceiling joists. If ceiling joists run parallel to frame, nail 2 x 4 cats, 2 ft. on centers, Illus. 31, between joists. This installation will not disturb waterproofing seal on wall or floor.

If you want to install a plasterboard ceiling, nail studs flatwise in position shown, Illus. 32. In this installation, the underside of plate, flush with bottom of joists, provides a nailer for ceiling panels. Note wall A. The shoe is installed edgewise. Studs are toenailed to shoe. Cats are nailed between joists to provide a nailer for ceiling panels on wall B.

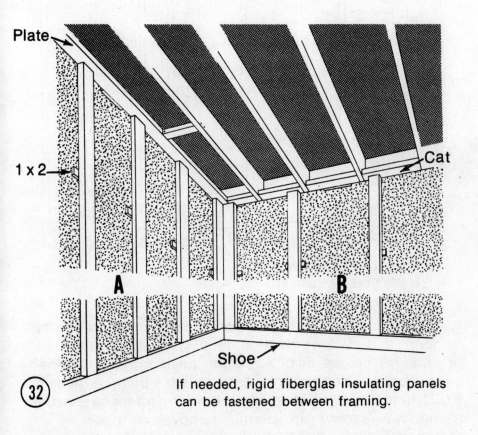

If needed, rigid fiberglas insulating panels can be fastened between framing.

Where a partition butts against an outside wall, nail 2 x 4 cats every 2 feet between studs to anchor end stud, Illus. 33. Or nail pieces of 2 x 4 flatwise as spacer blocks. Add an extra stud to form a pocket for end of partition.

BASEMENTS ABOVE GRADE

Where moisture or water seepage is no problem, 1 x 2, 5/4 x 3 bridging, 2 x 3 or 2 x 4 can be used to fur paneling from concrete block walls, Illus. 33.

Nail to walls with masonry nails. Space studs 16" on centers.

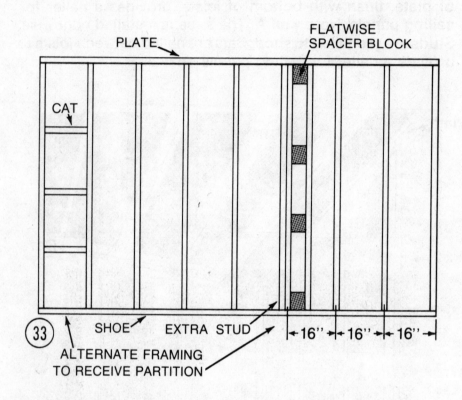

PLATE

FLATWISE
SPACER BLOCK

CAT

33

SHOE   EXTRA STUD   ←16"→←16"→←16"→

ALTERNATE FRAMING
TO RECEIVE PARTITION

As previously mentioned, position all outside wall frames ¾" from wall to provide ventilation. If wall contains a gas, electric or water meter, gas, oil or waste line, position studs to permit easy access. When prefinished panels are being applied to studs, hinge or screw every panel covering a service line. Use roundhead screws to permit removal in case of an emergency.

NOTE: Where a modernization requires street level entry and inside stairs, build stairs following directions starting on page 80, after applying paneling.

PARTITIONS

While most inside doors measure 2'8" x 6'8", frame rough opening to size required to fit door selected, Illus. 34. Your building material dealer will supply size of rough opening.

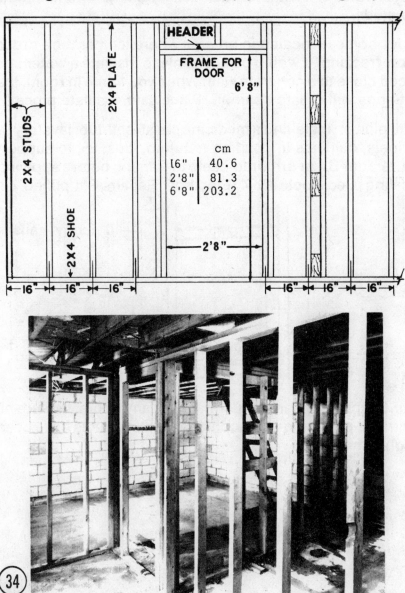

	cm
16"	40.6
2'8"	81.3
6'8"	203.2

34

When nailing studs to shoe and plate, use two 16 penny common nails at each joint. Buy No. 2 common lumber, or better, for partitions. Unless lumber is dry, it will twist when heat dries it out.

If you plan on installing a bathroom or kitchen that requires waste, water or vent lines, use 2 x 6 framing for shoe, plate and studs.

If your home is located in an area where temperature drops below freezing, it would be advisable to insulate a water line placed close to a concrete wall. When you frame in room, the partitions will create dead air. Place safe, insulate pipes.

If you plan on installing a medicine chest, bathtub, lavatory or cabinets, nail cats in position required, Illus. 35, to support fixture. Run BX or armored cable to framing before applying paneling. See Book #694, Electrical Repairs Simplified.

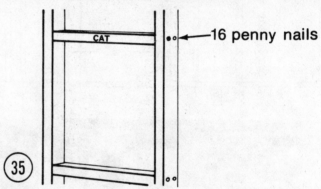

16 penny nails

Prior to applying paneling or hanging any doors, be sure all electrical, plumbing and additional heating ducts have been roughed in.

PANELING

¼" prefinished hardwood plywood and hardboard panels are available in many different wood grains, 4 x 7, 4 x 8 and 4 x 10'. These handsome panels permit amateurs to make like "pros" on their first paneling job.

First measure wall area to be covered, Illus. 42. Divide by 4' to estimate number of panels required. Place these in basement at the earliest possible time to acclimate before installation.

Panels can be installed with adhesive, color matched nails, or with a nailing machine called a Whammer, Illus. 36. These are great time savers.

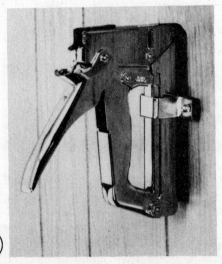

Panel adhesive simplifies installing panels on any firm, smooth and plumb surface. It sets fast and lessens possibility of panels loosening due to settling or moisture. DO NOT USE panel adhesive over loose paint, wallpaper, cracked or flaky plaster. DO NOT USE panel adhesive with veneer faced aluminum moldings.

Since a house settles, lumber shrinks and warps, you seldom find a corner square, floor or ceiling level throughout a room. For this reason, always measure distance from ceiling to floor. Do this at corner and again every four feet from corner. Cut panels ¼" less than overall height required.

Butt first panel snugly in corner, Illus. 37. Place level on outside edge and check to make certain panel is plumb. The ¼" allowance should permit positioning panel plumb.* Hold panel in plumb position with a couple of nails. Nails butt against edge of panel, not through panel. Or use 2 pieces of shingle as wedges, Illus. 37.

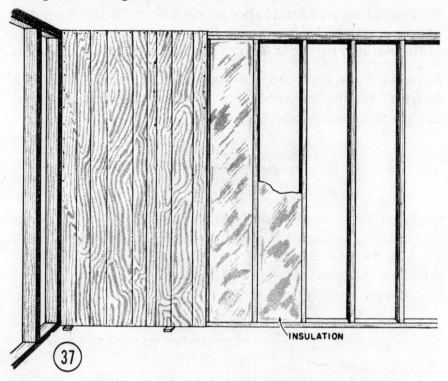

INSULATION

(37)

If a corner isn't plumb, fasten the panel temporarily in plumb position and scribe edge to corner. Keep point of scriber following corner, Illus. 38, pencil on panel. A charcoal white pencil (available in art supply stores) will mark without damaging a prefinished panel. Remove panel, saw or plane along scribed line. Replace panel. Check with level. If necessary, scribe panel to ceiling. When panel is cut to fit corner, remove panel and apply a single bead of adhesive the full length of each stud. Follow adhesive manufacturer's directions. Apply adhesive across shoe and plate.

Book #605 How to Apply Paneling contains information covering many special situations.

*NOTE: If corner is more than slightly out of plumb, it may be necessary to cut panel ⅜" less than overall height.

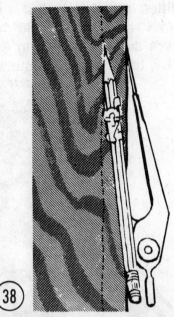

(38)

Replace panel in position, temporarily drive three 6 penny finishing nails about 8" apart along top edge of panel, Illus. 39. The nails act as a hinge. Press panel firmly in position, then pull out and block bottom edge 8 to 10" from wall. This permits air to set adhesive until it gets tacky.**

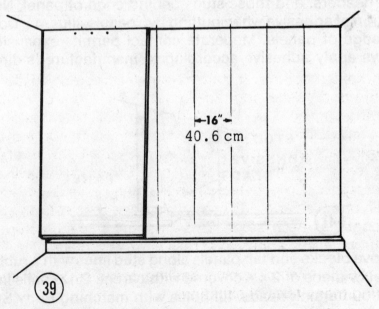

←16"→
40.6 cm

(39)

**Some adhesive does not require this step.

Panel adhesive simplifies installation, but it should only be applied in temperatures ranging from 60° and up. Some adhesive manufacturers suggest applying 3" strips of ⅛" thick adhesive every 6", to all intermediate studs, Illus. 40.

Apply a continuous ⅛" bead of adhesive along shoe, plate, cats, headers, and those studs behind edge of panel. Note position of adhesive when butting two panels, Illus. 41. Don't jam edge of panels. Moderate contact permits expansion. Always apply adhesive according to manufacturer's directions.

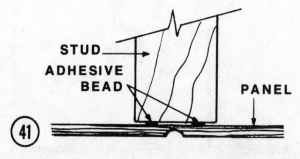

STUD
ADHESIVE
BEAD
PANEL

Remove blocks and tap panels along stud lines with a rubber mallet or piece of 2 x 4 covered with carpet. Drive nails in at top, countersink heads, fill holes with matching Putty Stik.

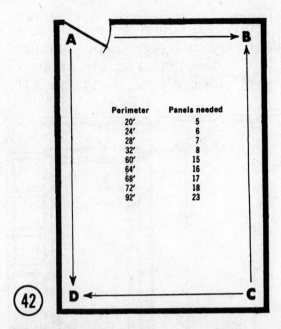

Perimeter	Panels needed
20′	5
24′	6
28′	7
32′	8
60′	15
64′	16
68′	17
72′	18
92′	23

(42)

When first panel is plumb, it simplifies installing other panels. Start at A and work toward B, Illus. 42, cutting last panel size to fit. Start at C, work toward B and D. Fit each in position before applying adhesive. If panel doesn't butt squarely along edge, you can get a tighter joint by planing edge, Illus. 43.

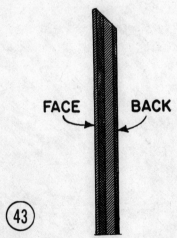

FACE   BACK

(43)

Always plan application so full panels butt together in the most prominent corner of the room. When panels have to be cut, butt cut panels together in the least conspicuous corner.

When a panel requires a cutout for part or all of a door, window or outlet box; plumb panel in position tight against ceiling. Draw top and bottom line of opening. Measure distance to edge of previously installed panel A, Illus. 44.

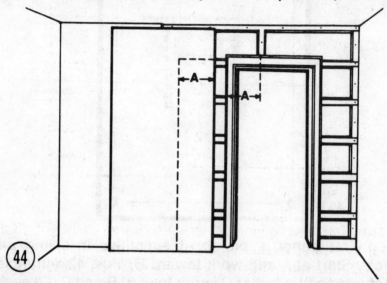

Drill a line of ⅛" holes at diagonal corners on inside of line drawn for a window or door, Illus. 45. This permits inserting a keyhole or saber saw.

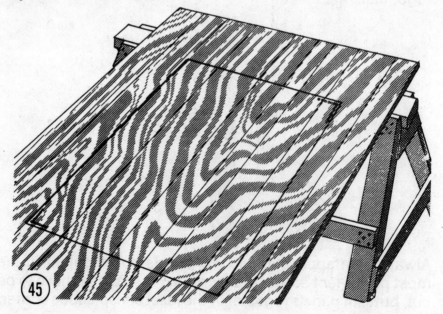

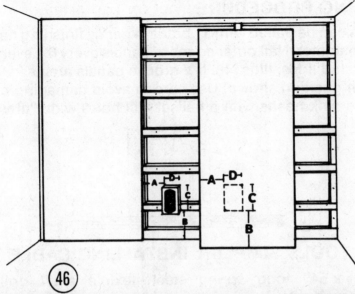

(46)

To cut a panel for a wall outlet, raise panel to height off floor equal to other panels. Measure and mark height of opening A,B,C,D, Illus. 46. Drill ½" holes in position indicated, Illus. 47. Use a keyhole or saber saw to cut opening for box.

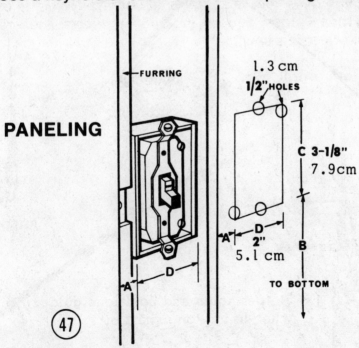

PANELING

FURRING

1.3 cm
1/2"HOLES

C 3-1/8"
7.9cm

A
D
2"
5.1 cm

B

TO BOTTOM

(47)

NAILING PROCEDURE

Panels can be nailed with 1" brads, 4 penny finishing nails or the Whammer. Nail outer edges of panels every 6", every 12" along stud lines, Illus. 48. If V groove panels are used, drive nails in position shown. Use care to avoid damaging panel. Countersink heads with a nailset. Fill holes with Putty Stik.

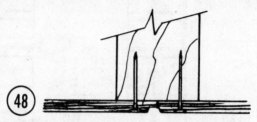

NEW TOOLS SIMPLIFY INSTALLING CABLE

The ⅜ x 54" long spring steel flexible shaft drill, an alignment guide, plus a wire gripper turn amateurs into pros. The gripper, Illus. 49, permits using the drill as a snake to draw cable through the wall.

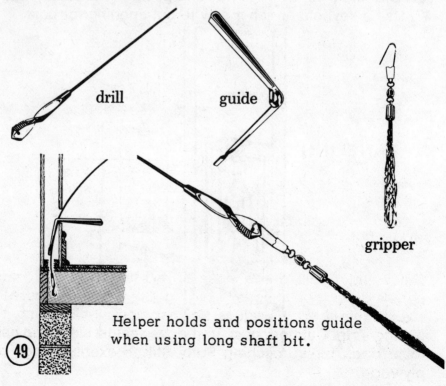

drill

guide

gripper

Helper holds and positions guide when using long shaft bit.

PANELING AROUND A RECESSED WINDOW

If you panel a basement wall containing a recessed window, and want to apply hardwood paneling to sides of recess, do this.

Apply furring to wall, Illus. 33,50, and around recess, Illus. 51. Cut and toenail 1 x 2 fillers A, Illus. 50,51, in position shown. Cut wall panels to project ¼" beyond edge of recess all the way around.

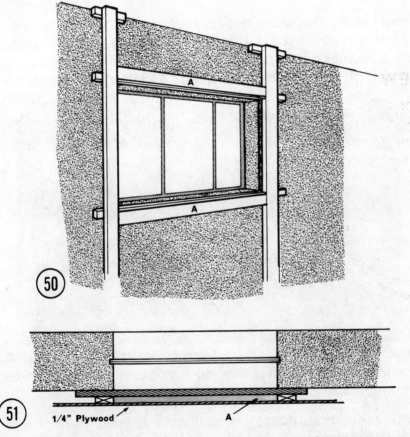

Cut ¼" plywood to size sides of recess require. Nail side panels in position to edge of furring. Cut ceiling of recess to size required so it wedges against sides. Nail ceiling to furring strip. Cut bottom so it wedges against sides and nail to furring. Apply matching Putty Stik to exposed edge of plywood.

47

HOW TO LAY FLOOR TILE

These directions simplify laying 9 x 9" asphalt and vinyl tiles over wood, plywood or hardboard. Since there are many manufacturers, and most supply adhesive, buy adhesive when you buy tiles, and always follow their directions. To add prestige plus an easy to maintain floor, consider quarry or ceramic tile. Complete directions are detailed in Book #606. Those who want to lay wall to wall carpeting should read Book #683.

If floor is firm, but uneven, or slopes, you can fill and smooth low spots with latex floor underlayment. This can be spread from a feather edge to 5/16" thick in one coat, Illus. 52. Any number of coats can be applied. It dries to a hard base, perfect for ceramic or asphalt tile floor. Follow manufacturer's directions when applying to underlayment selected.

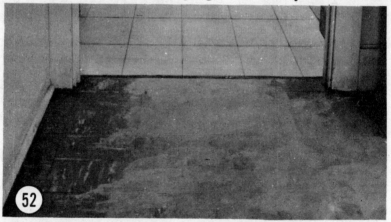

Latex underlayment can be used to level floor covered by plywood. Carpet adhesives do not bond to latex underlayment.

While most manufacturers sell an adhesive that permits laying tile directly to wood floors, hardboard or plywood, some recommend bonding #15 felt over concrete.

All surfaces must be smooth, level, all cracks filled and smooth. Floors must be free of dust, paint, wax, other finishes, etc. Wash floor after leveling to make certain all dust and dirt has been eliminated.

If manufacturer recommends laying felt over a wood floor, use #15 felt. Lay crosswise to flooring. Don't overlap. Make a neat butt joint. Spread felt paste or adhesive with a notched spreader, Illus. 53. Unroll and press felt down to eliminate air pockets.

A — CHALK   D — NOTCHED SPREADER
B — CHALK LINE   E — AWL
C — MASON'S TROWEL   F — LINOLEUM KNIFE

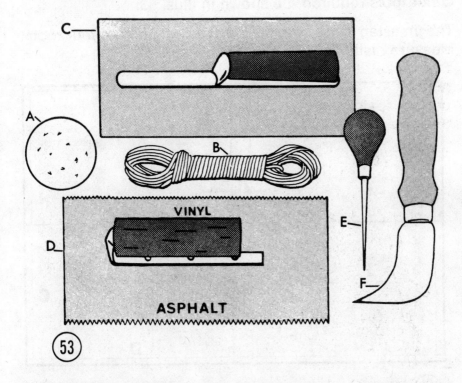

VINYL

ASPHALT

53

Do a little at a time. Rent a floor roller to smooth and bond felt to floor or use a rolling pin. The felt underlayment must be absolutely smooth. Ridges or creases must be avoided. No felt is required when plywood or hardboard underlayment is used.

Asphalt tile comes in 9 x 9" size, ⅛ and 3/16" thick. 12 x 12" is also available. ⅛" thick is packed 80 pieces to a carton; 3/16" thick is packed 54 pieces to a carton.

Do not attempt to lay tiles in a cold room or on a cold floor. Room temperature should be 72° or higher. Place tiles in room where they are to be installed several days ahead of time to make certain all are room temperature when laid.

Asphalt tiles can be cut by scoring a line across top and bottom with an awl. Snap along scored line. Apply heat from a propane torch to cut odd shapes. Merely warm tile, don't burn, and it will cut easily. Always cut with finish face up. Other tools required are shown in Illus. 53.

The first step is to locate the exact center point of your room. Measure distance A and B, Illus. 54.

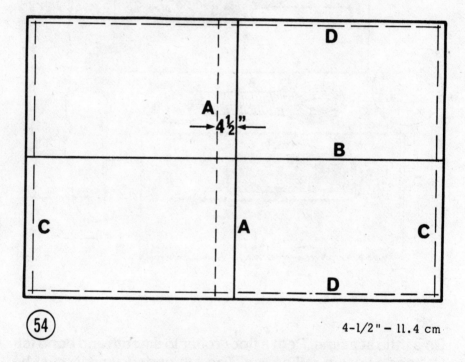

(54)

4-1/2" – 11.4 cm

Start at center and lay tiles without adhesive, Illus. 55, to determine how many full tiles can be laid. Borders should be at least one half tile width, or wider. If border C is 2" or less, or more than 8", move line A 4½" closer to C. Relay tiles. Border C should be equal. Follow same procedure, move line B 4½" closer to D to obtain proper size borders. Border D should also be equal but need not be the width of C, Illus. 56.

50

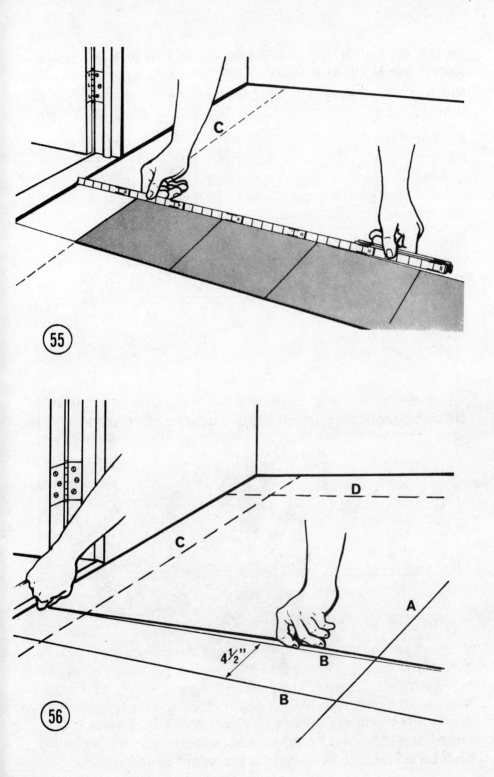

(55)

C

(56)

D

C

A

$4\frac{1}{2}''$

B

B

Butt tile to door sill. If opening doesn't have a sill, nail or screw metal sill in position, Illus. 57.

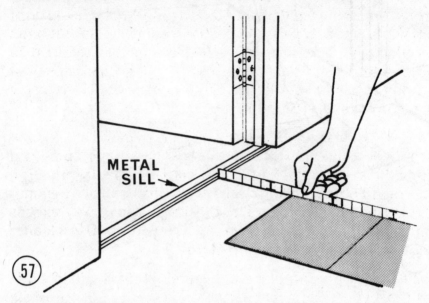

METAL
SILL →

57

Start at center and spread adhesive following manufacturer's directions, Illus. 58. Do one quarter of a room at a time.

58

Use a notched trowel, Illus. 53. Hold at about 45° angle. Use a sweeping motion. Spread adhesive evenly, follow manufacturer's directions explicitly. Don't leave any globs. If you do, it will work up between tiles. Allow adhesive to set time manufacturer recommends. While it will usually set up in 15 minutes to a half hour, don't rush. It should feel tacky but shouldn't stick to your finger. Since some adhesive remains alive for days, there's no rush.

Start at center and place, don't slide, tiles in position. Make certain tiles line up with chalk lines. All tiles should be laid with edges flush and tight and with pattern in direction required to obtain design desired. Use the head of a hammer to rub edge of tile for a smooth joint. Wipe away excess adhesive (if you should have any) as you go. Use cleaner recommended by tile manufacturer.

To fit tile for border, place a loose tile X, Illus. 59, in exact position over tile adjacent to border. Place tile Y on top of tile X. Butt tile Y against wall or cabinet. Draw line on tile X. Cut tile X to size required.

Use X as a border tile.

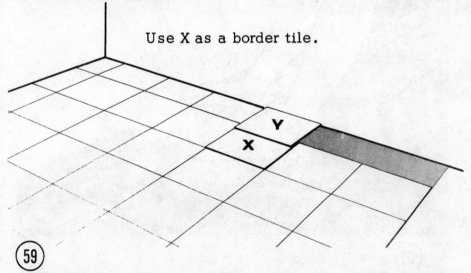

(59)

Follow same procedure in fitting each piece of border tile. Since tile Y will get dirty, use it over and over. Left over pieces of border tile can be cut to size required to cover kickboard on base cabinet.

Roll each section of floor with a floor roller before starting next quarter. If you have to make odd shaped cutouts for pipes, first make a paper pattern. When it's right, trace it on tile. Heat tile then cut to shape required. Tin snips frequently simplify cutting certain shapes. Household scissors can be used to cut vinyl tiles.

In most cases you can pry up a radiator or range to slip tile under or cut tile to fit. Use a piece of 2 x 4 and a prybar. In this case it will be necessary to apply adhesive to tile. Most gas and electric ranges can be raised sufficiently to permit inserting tile in position.

Note: Matching base is readily available. This permits covering joint between last tile and base cabinet. Use adhesive manufacturer recommends when installing base, Illus. 60.

60

Many manufacturers sell colorful tile inserts and strips that can be worked into a floor. These add a note of distinction and are well worth installing.

Large size border tiles are also available. These permit fitting border tile in area around door casing and sill, Illus. 57. Use a piece of 1 x 3, or small roller, to firmly press border tile in position.

When border tile butts against an irregularity, scribe border to shape.

Cut border tile a hair oversize to fit snugly in position. Heat edge that butts against baseboard over a propane torch. Use a small roller or piece of 1 x 3 to press soft tile into position.

HANG DOORS

Use 3½ x 3½" loose pin butt hinges. Mortise hinge in door 6" down from top, 8½" up from bottom, third hinge at center. Place hinge in position and mark outline on edge of door. Using a 1" chisel, make cuts to depth equal to thickness of hinge leaf, Illus. 61, 62. Chisel out mortise, Illus. 63, and fasten leaf, Illus. 64.

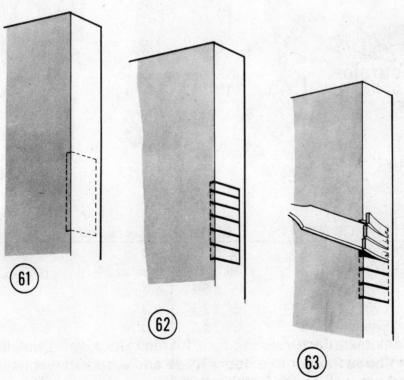

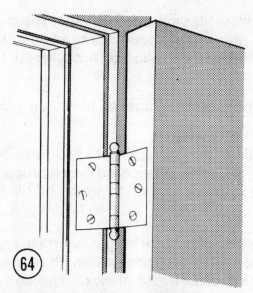

(64)

PREFINISHED WOOD MOLDINGS

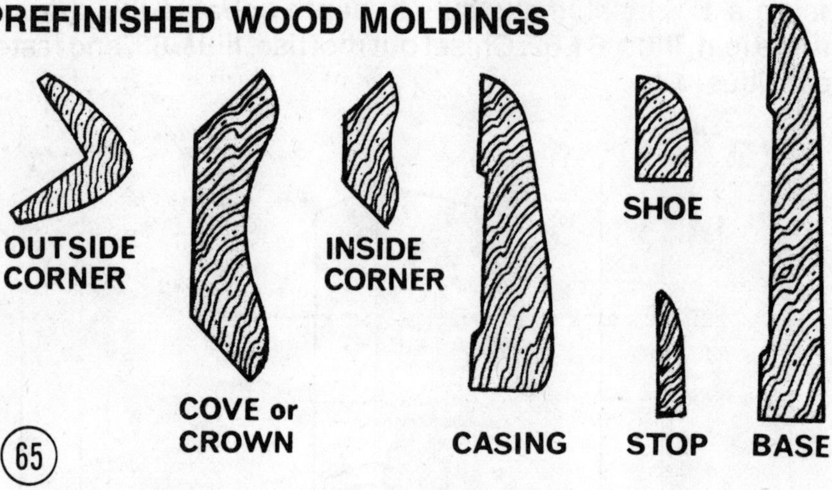

OUTSIDE CORNER

COVE or CROWN

INSIDE CORNER

CASING

SHOE

STOP

BASE

(65)

DESCRIPTION	SIZE	metric	LTH. metric
Shoe	⅝″ x ⁵⁄₁₆″	1.6 x .8 cm	10′ — 304.8 cm
Stop	1⁵⁄₁₆″ x ⁵⁄₁₆″	3.3 x .8	10′
Casing	½″ x 2¼″	1.3 x 5.7	7′ — 213.4
Casing	½″ x 2¼″	1.3 x 5.7	10′
Base	¹³⁄₃₂″ x 3″	1.0 x 7.6	10′
Outside Corner	⅞″ x ⅞″	2.2 x 2.2	8′ — 243.8
Inside Corner	¾″ x ¾″	1.9 x 1.9	8′
Cove	⁹⁄₁₆″ x 2¼″	1.4 x 5.7	10′

56

Prefinished wood moldings, Illus. 65, simplify trimming walls, ceiling, doors and windows. The shoe can be used with or without base. Use the stop and casing to trim a window or door, Illus. 66. Casing can also be used as a chair rail. Use corner bead as an outside corner. Note inside and outside corner moldings, Illus. 67.

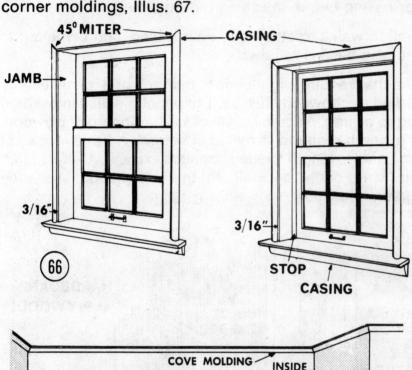

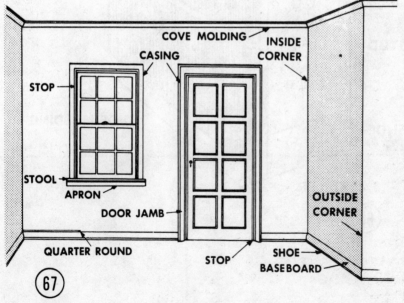

The cove or crown molding is frequently used at ceiling. When applying casing to windows and doors, miter cut top ends 45° and cut to length required. Apply adhesive to miter joint, then nail casings in place with 4 penny finishing nails. The miter can be touched up with matching Putty Stik. Install door casing before installing base molding.

If wall to wall carpeting is to be installed, butt carpeting to panel. No base is required.

Walls that require slightly more than a 7 or 8' panel can be handled as shown in Illus. 68. The panel is nailed in position snug to ceiling. A scrap length of ¼'' hardboard or plywood, cut to width required, is nailed at bottom. A 6 or 8'' base cut from panel to length needed, is nailed in place. Always match grain with panel on wall. In this installation use shoe molding, Illus. 65.

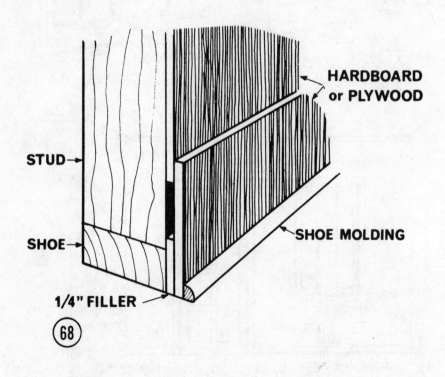

HARDBOARD or PLYWOOD

STUD→

SHOE→

SHOE MOLDING

1/4" FILLER

68

ENCLOSING PIPES, GIRDERS, HEATING DUCTS

A steel beam or girder can be enclosed in this manner. Nail 1 x 2 A alongside girder, Illus. 69. Cut ¼'' plywood B to width and length required, Illus. 70. Nail B to 1 x 2 C spaced as shown. Cut ¼'' plywood D to width and length required. Nail D to C. Raise assembled enclosure and nail D to A.

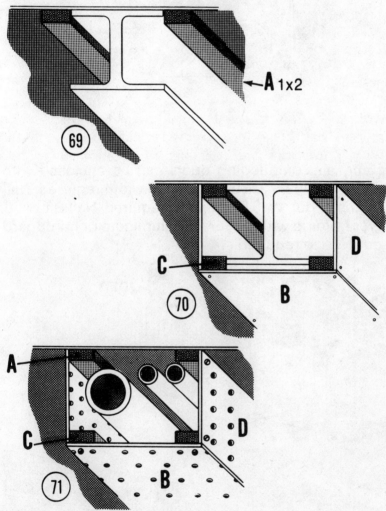

Follow same procedure when enclosing pipes and valves, Illus. 71, with the following changes. Pipes that contain shut off valves require inspection. Pipes also need air. Use pegboard for B and D. Screw D to A so entire enclosure can be removed.

Illus. 72 shows another way of enclosing pipe. Nail D to E and C. Screw B to C. Screw E to bottom of joist.

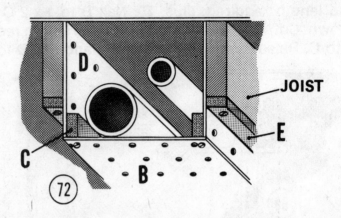

Heating and air conditioning ducts can be enclosed with framing shown, Illus. 73. Build frame to width required. Nail 1 x 2 A to joists. Cut 1 x 3 B to length required. Nail B to A, C to B. Cover framing with perforated aluminum or hardboard panels cut to size required.

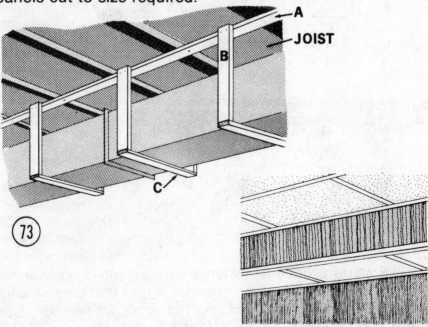

If joists run parallel to duct, nail B to joists.

Posts in a basement should be enclosed, Illus. 74,75. Nail 1 x 6 or width required to 1 x 2. Space 1 x 2 every 2 ft. full height of column. Cut panel to size required. Apply corner bead, base and shoe, or shoe molding. Miter ends of shoe. Use matching trim at ceiling.

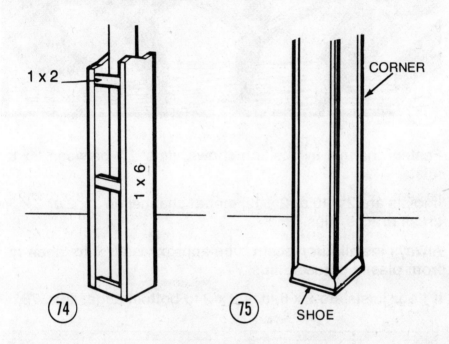

INSTALLATION OF FLUORESCENT CHANNEL BETWEEN FLOOR JOISTS

Illus. 76, 77, 78, 79.

First decide whether you want to recess fluorescent lighting between joists, Illus. 76; recess spotlights or conventional fixtures. Book #694 Electrical Repairs Simplified provides considerable detail concerning the many different ways a luminous ceiling, luminous ceiling panel, and luminous walls can be installed.

If bridging between floor joists, Illus. 76, prevents installing channel within area selected, remove and fasten bridging outside light cavity.

61

Fasten channel in position shown, Illus. 77, between 2 x 8 joists.

If joists are 2 x 10 or 2 x 12, mount channel on 1 x 2 or 2 x 3 cross braces, Illus. 78.

Always install fluorescent tube approximately 3 to 5'' away from plastic diffuser, Illus. 77.

If floor joists are 2 x 6, nail 2 x 2 to bottom edge, Illus. 79.

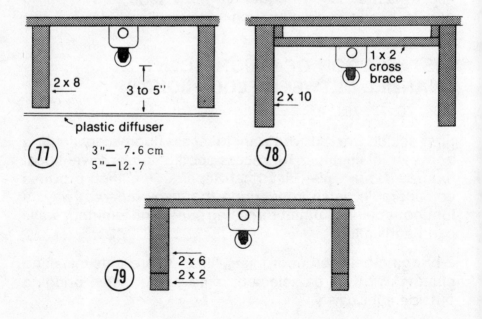

2 x 8
3 to 5''
plastic diffuser
77
3''— 7.6 cm
5''—12.7

1 x 2 cross brace
2 x 10
78

2 x 6
2 x 2
79

HOW TO INSTALL A SUSPENDED CEILING

Most suspended ceilings consist of three aluminum components — a pre-punched wall angle, Illus. 80, main runner and cross tees, plus 2 x 2 and 2 x 4 ceiling panels.

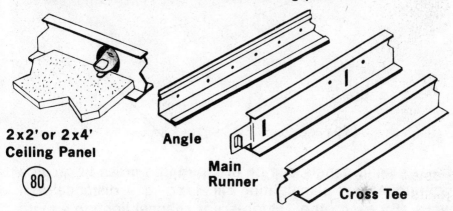

**2 x 2' or 2 x 4'
Ceiling Panel**

Angle

**Main
Runner**

Cross Tee

80

Using the grid on page 98, make a sketch to ascertain best way to run main runner and cross tees, Illus. 81. Does a 2 x 2 panel make a better looking ceiling than a 2 x 4 panel? Or should you cut border panels to one size and go clear round the room with this width panel? Using the layout chart, allow each square to equal one foot. Indicate all lighting panels, heat and air conditioning louvers.

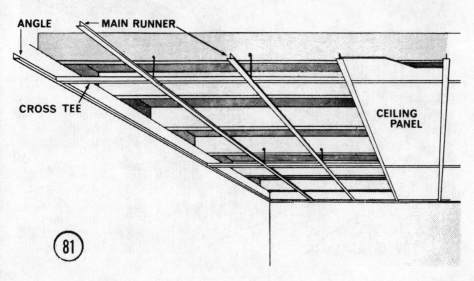

ANGLE — MAIN RUNNER

CROSS TEE

CEILING
PANEL

81

When planning position of main runners and cross tees, give priority to columns. Position framing so column goes through ceiling panel, Illus. 82. This might necessitate a slightly smaller border on one side.

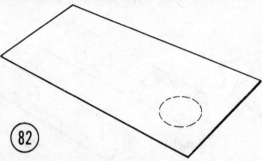

Clear plastic panels can be dropped into areas to provide lighting. Always plan lighting panels an equal distance from walls and each other. Fluorescent channel lighting should never be installed in ceilings less than 7'6" in height.

Installation starts by snapping a level chalk line clear around room at height selected for the finished ceiling, Illus. 83. Since both the floor and existing ceiling may slope, use a 4' level and a chalk line to establish a level line.

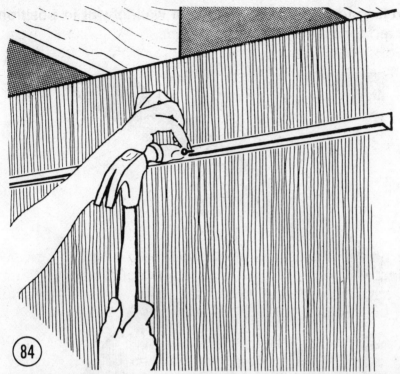

Nail angle molding to wall end to end all around room, Illus. 84, at height selected for ceiling. Using grid, decide what size panels you can install and where each will be located. Position of main runners is dependent on the 2'0'' width or length of each panel.

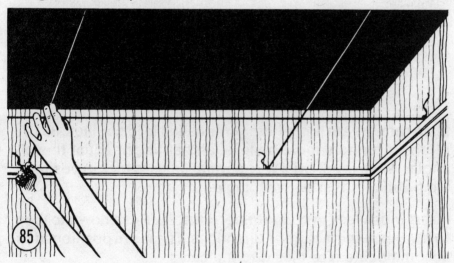

Stretch guide lines, Illus, 85, from wall-to-wall in position selected for main runners.

86

Main runners are hung from wires nailed to joists, Illus. 86,87. All main runners must be level and at height equal to wall angle. When level, twist wire several times to lock in position. Main runners rest on wall angle.

Insert cross tees in main runner, Illus. 88. Push down to lock following manufacturer's directions. These are positioned to accommodate size tiles grid indicates.

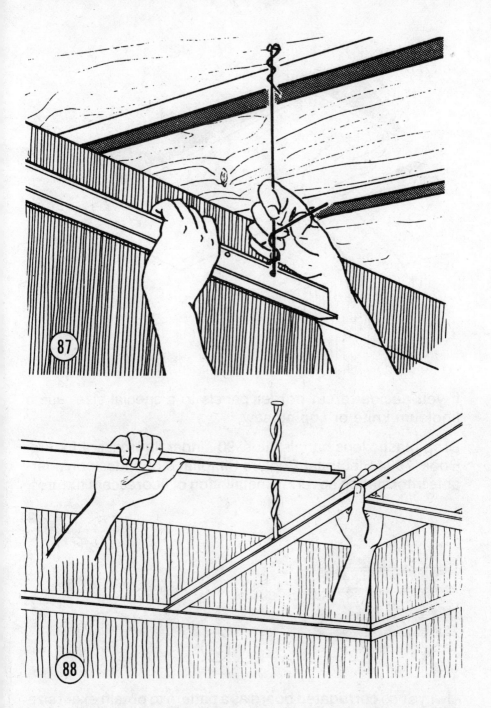

Tilt ceiling panels into each opening and drop into place, Illus. 89. Lock panel with tabs in frame, Illus. 80, when manufacturer provides same.

If you decide to cut border panels to a special size, use a linoleum knife or coping saw.

Drop plastic lens panels, Illus. 90, under fluorescent fixture. Book #694 Electrical Repairs Simplified provides considerable information covering installation of fluorescent fixtures.

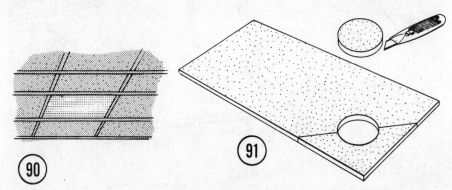

Always use corrugated board as a pattern to obtain exact size and location for opening for a column, Illus. 86. When it's OK, trace and cut opening. This can be made with a utility knife, Illus. 91.

HOW TO INSTALL AN OUTSIDE DOOR

Those interested in converting a basement into living space for a relative or tenant must consider privacy an important part of the plan. Unless both families can live their own lives and keep out of each other's way, the added income loses much of its lure.

Due to a frightening rise in crime, solvent singles search for safe living space. They are perfectly willing to pay top dollar for the security they gain from living under the same roof with a normal family. Since very few will rent space where a metal enclosure, Illus. 18, provides entry, an alternative is a grade level entry door, Illus. 92, with stairs inside. This should be first choice for those starting to convert a basement into an income producing apartment.

(92)

Where an outside entry is presently covered with a metal enclosure, a charming alternative can be a walk through greenhouse entry, Illus. 93. Complete directions for building on foundation shown, Illus. 2A, are described in Book #611 How to Build a Greenhouse. Note size of foundation required. If this entry is of interest, check location of existing basement stairs to see if space permits a slightly larger foundation. Also give some thought to making the greenhouse longer. Many renting a basement apartment are happy to pay extra for the privilege of using a greenhouse.

Selecting a location for an outside door convenient to either the street or to a driveway, depends on the following. The door must be positioned where C, Illus. 94, is 36" or more from foundation wall.

While a door can be cut into any blank wall, or a first floor window can be removed to install a door, select a location that doesn't contain any pipes, heating duct or electrical conduit. While most walls will contain some BX, this can be rerouted without too much trouble.

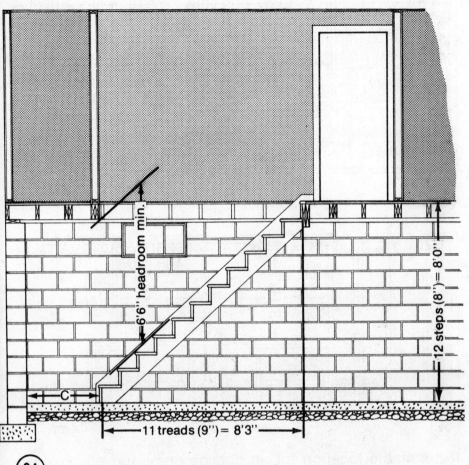

6'6" headroom min.

12 steps (8") = 8'0"

C

11 treads (9") = 8'3"

(94)

Those planning a rental apartment with a kitchen and bath should note location of supply and drainage lines. Making the shortest possible run to supply and waste lines cuts costs.

If space selected for stairs along an outside wall runs parallel to existing floor joists, Illus. 95, it usually requires cutting two or three joists. If joists run perpendicular to space selected, Illus. 96, it usually requires cutting seven joists.

Go into basement and note direction of floor joists. If a basement window is in position shown, Illus. 94, it's a plus.

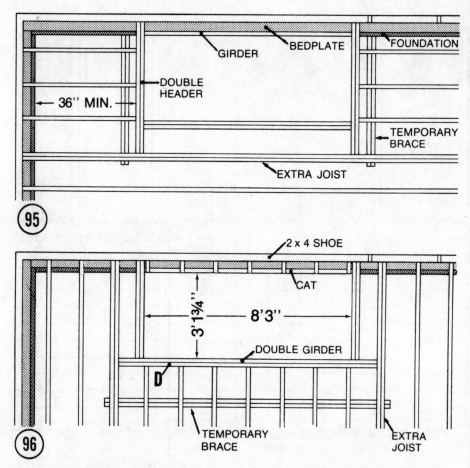

GIRDER BEDPLATE FOUNDATION

DOUBLE HEADER

← 36" MIN. →

TEMPORARY BRACE

EXTRA JOIST

95

2 x 4 SHOE

CAT

3' 1¾"   8'3"

DOUBLE GIRDER

D

TEMPORARY BRACE

EXTRA JOIST

96

If a suitable location for an outside entry doesn't provide quite enough space for stairs straight down, consider two alternatives. Your building materials retailer can lay out stairs with a one or two step platform landing, Illus. 97; winder stairs, Illus. 98; or you can buy a prefabricated metal or wood spiral stairway, Illus. 99, that requires minimum space.

Note what's below area selected for stairs. Are floor joists free of hot and cold water pipes, heating duct, etc.? Do joists run parallel to rectangle drawn for stair opening, or do they run across? Does basement floor permit erecting a partition alongside, and under end of stairs? Does the foundation wall finish flush with side of opening, or does it project into area needed for stairs?

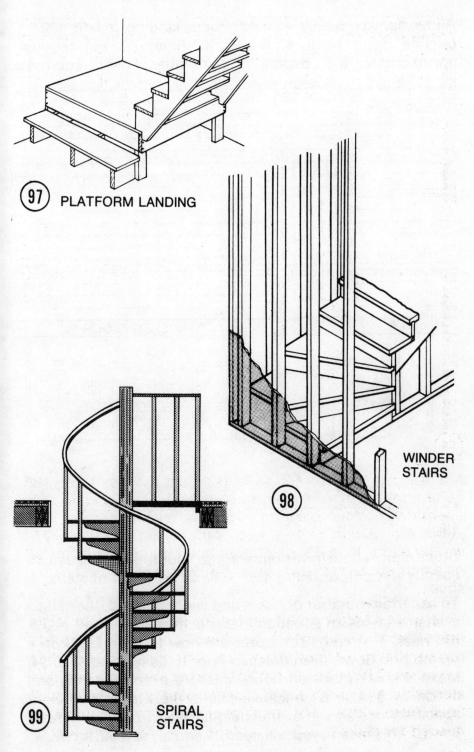

97 PLATFORM LANDING

98 WINDER STAIRS

99 SPIRAL STAIRS

Allow approximately 42 x 42" for a landing inside a 2'8"
outside door. Note A, Illus. 100. Space B will require
approximately 8'3", depending on number of risers required.

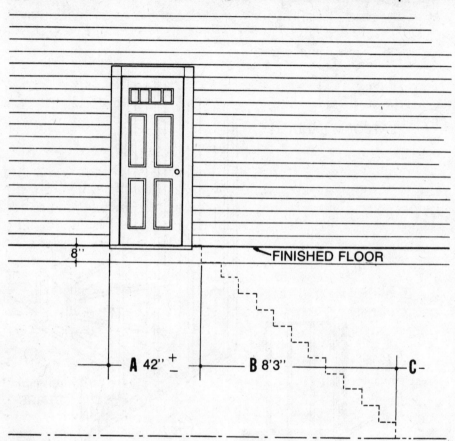

FINISHED FLOOR

8"

A 42" $\pm$ B 8'3"   C

(100)

Stock stairs come in various widths. Your retailer will usually
specify a rough opening 1⅜" wider than width of stairs.

To ascertain number of risers and width of tread, the skilled
craftsman uses an equation that specifies 2R + one T = 25.
(R - riser, T - tread). To appreciate how this works, drop a
plumb bob down from finished floor to basement, Illus. 94.
Make a chalk mark on floor. Measure exact distance and
divide by 8. Use 8" because this is the maximum height
specified for risers. If overall height measures 96", divide by
8 = 12. This means you will need 12 equally spaced steps.

An 8" step, or riser as its commonly called, includes a 1⅛" thick tread, 6⅞" riser*. Thickness of existing finished flooring, plus subflooring frequently measures 1⅛". Buy stock nosing, Illus. 122. If overall height can't be divided by 8, try 7⅞, 7¾, etc., etc., or absorb a 5, 6 or 7" difference in a starting platform.

To determine width of tread, add two R, subtract from 25 and you have Y — width of tread. If R = 8, two R = 16. This indicates a 9" wide tread.

Headroom on stairs should not be less than 6'6". Stock stairs are available in 30 to 48" width. Those who plan on having retailer install an assembled stairway can still save a bundle by preparing the opening. Make certain assembled stairs can be snaked into house and in position. Those buying prefabricated components can assemble stairs in place.

When you have selected exact location for a landing and stairway, drive a 16 penny nail through finished flooring at each corner. Only drive nail sufficient distance to project below subflooring. This helps locate opening from below.

After selecting exact location for stairs, you can start to install an outside door. If a window is in position selected for a door, Illus. 101, measure distance inside house from floor to sash X. Go outside and measure an equal distance down from same point on sash. Draw a line, Illus. 102. This indicates level of floor on outside.

Ask retailer for rough opening size of an exterior door frame. While these come in various widths, we don't recommend any smaller than 2'8". Buy frame and prehung door.

Use a level to draw plumb lines. Before drilling holes needed for a keyhole, compass or reciprocating saw, Illus. 9, make certain no heating or water lines or electrical conduit cross opening. Note location of wall outlets. Go into basement. See if BX serving outlet runs up from basement. If it doesn't, the box is probably connected to another wall outlet with conduit through studs.

*Also available 1 1/16" tread, 6 15/16" riser.

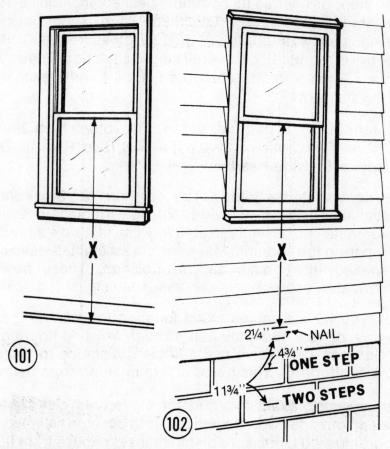

101

102

2¼" NAIL

4¾" ONE STEP

1 13¾" TWO STEPS

An outside door sill usually requires approximately 2¼" of space below finished flooring. Measure down 2¼", or distance retailer specifies for frame he sells, and draw a line, Illus. 102.

Working on the inside, remove window stops, Illus. 103, and sash. Pry up top trim, then side trim B. Remove apron D. Knock up and remove sill C. Still working from inside, place a short block of 2 x 4 against bottom of window frame. With hammer, drive frame out just enough to loosen nails. Go outside, drive frame back, pull out projecting nails. Use care and pry out frame with a wrecking bar. Saw exterior siding, sub-sheathing, inside plaster or plasterboard, down alongside stud to finished floor and remove. Saw shoe and knock out framing between opening, Illus. 104, 105.

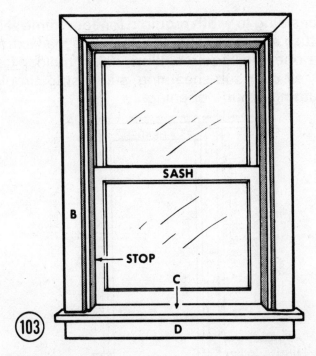

(103)

SASH

B

STOP

C

D

If builder left out short stud A, Illus. 104, nail one in position.

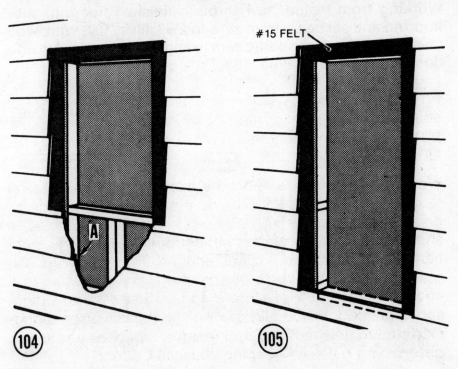

#15 FELT

A

(104)

(105)

Cut exterior siding to width required for door frame selected. Do not disturb #15 felt or sub-sheathing. Toenail extra studs in position opening requires, Illus. 106. If builder failed to apply #15 felt over sub-sheathing, staple strips in place to cover sheathing around opening.

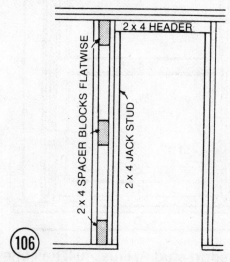

106

Working from inside, saw through finished flooring, subflooring and sill beam from zero to 2¼", Illus. 107. With wide chisel or hatchet, chop sill beam to angle required for outside door sill and frame, Illus. 108.

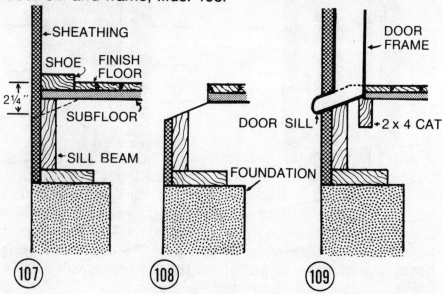

107 108 109

Nail 2 x 4 between floor joists to support edge of floor, Illus. 109. Plumb frame in opening. Check to make certain it's level. Nail frame in place with 8 penny finishing nails. Countersink heads. Fill holes with putty. Nail siding along cut edge. Calk joint.

If you purchase an outside door frame without a prehung door, install door following directions outlined on page 55.

BUILD OUTSIDE STEP

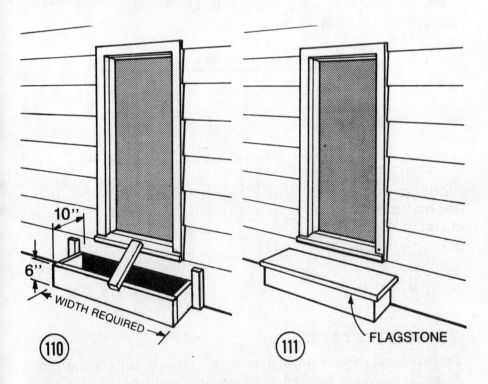

If your entry requires building an outside step, follow this procedure. Excavate to below frost level and fill with rock. Cover clapboard or shingle below door sill with #15 roofing felt or ½" asphalt impregnated board. Build form to size shown, Illus. 110. Do not drive nails all the way in. Fill form with concrete consisting of one part cement, three parts sand, four parts small gravel. Fill form. Tamp it with a 2 x 4. Level surface, then score before it sets.

Allow concrete to set three days. Mix one part cement to two parts sand. Cover step with sufficient mortar to bed flagstone. Position flagstone, Illus. 111. Allow to set undisturbed before carefully pulling nails and removing form. Face ends and front of step with mortar consisting of one part cement to two parts of finely screened sand.

If height to door sill requires two steps, consider laying a raised terrace plus one step,Illus.111A. Where space permits, a brick or flagstone terrace adds charm to your entry. Put in footing and pour step before laying terrace. Book #668 explains how to lay a brick terrace.

FIRST FLOOR PARTITION

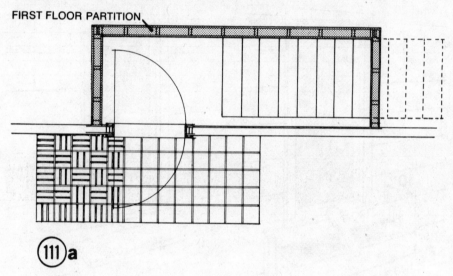

(111)a

TO BUILD STAIRS

Since most home improvement centers sell completely assembled stairs as well as all components, we recommend buying. Be sure to ask retailer to check location you have selected and to recommend rough opening he requires. When you have the opening ready, two men can raise and install stairs in very little time, providing they can get them into the basement.

If shipping costs for an assembled stairway are excessive, or you can't get one into the basement, buy precut parts and assemble it yourself.

80

Layout opening to overall size retailer specifies, Illus. 112.
Regardless of whether an opening for stairs is cut the long
way parallel to joists, or at right angle, it's necessary to first
support joists a short distance from where they are to be cut.
Allow yourself working space.

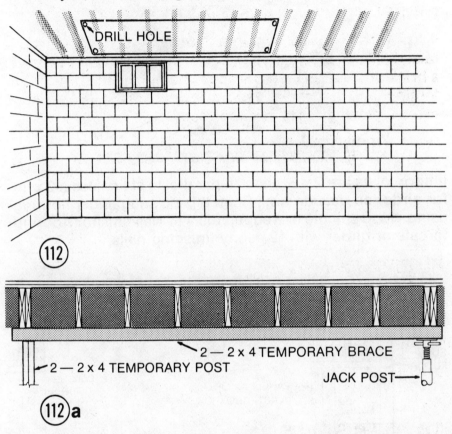

Drill a hole through floor at each corner of proposed
opening, or drive a 16 penny nail through floor so you can see
position of opening from basement. Spike two 2 x 4's
together for a brace. Toenail to bottom of joists, Illus. 112A.
Support these with double 2 x 4 posts or screw jacks. Force
studs in position under brace so it eliminates any play.

When cutting an opening, allow existing flooring to project
over edge so it finishes flush with furring applied to
foundation side, and flush with double girder on other side
and with headers, Illus. 113. Mark and saw joists for opening.

One way to saw joists to length that allows flooring to project proper distance is to drill a hole in position required, Illus. 112B. Using a level, draw a plumb line. Insert saber or reciprocating saw blade and saw joist.

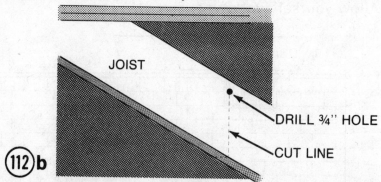

JOIST

DRILL ¾" HOLE

CUT LINE

(112) b

If floor joists are 2 x 8, and run parallel to stairs, use a 2 x 10 for girder on outside wall. Shim this up snug under flooring using wood shingle or wedge, Illus. 113. Nail finished flooring to cats or girder with 12 penny finishing nails.

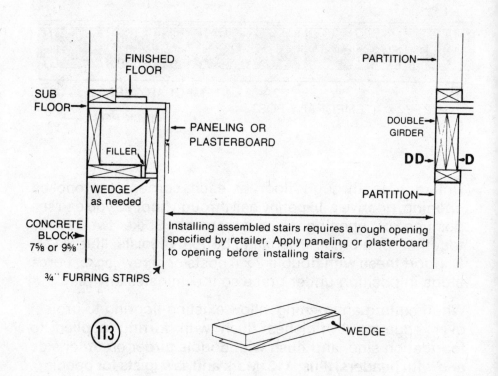

FINISHED FLOOR

PARTITION →

SUB FLOOR →

← PANELING OR PLASTERBOARD

DOUBLE → GIRDER

FILLER

DD → ← D

WEDGE as needed

PARTITION →

CONCRETE BLOCK →
7⅝ or 9⅝"

Installing assembled stairs requires a rough opening specified by retailer. Apply paneling or plasterboard to opening before installing stairs.

¾" FURRING STRIPS

(113)

WEDGE

Cats between joists, Illus. 114, can be same width as joists, or one size larger, Illus. 96. Double girder and headers should be width of joist. NOTE: If retailer suggests a wider header to receive stringers, install same.

Toenail cats to joists. Nail through D into ends of joists; through joist into ends of D. Spike D D in place. Toenail headers to girder. Insert extra joists where shown.

Nail single joist hanger X to each joist, Illus. 114A; nail double joist hanger Y to each header and double girder, Illus. 114. Nail finished flooring to cats, girder and headers with 8 penny finishing nails. Countersink heads.

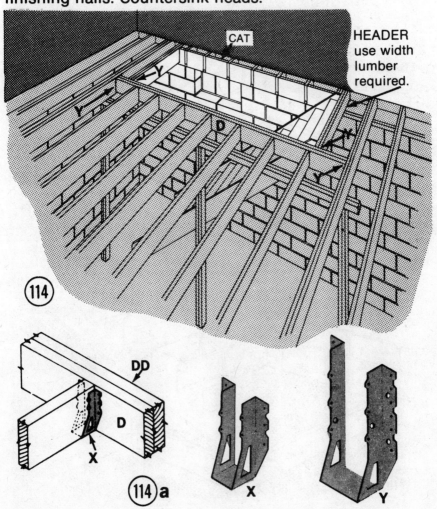

CAT

HEADER use width lumber required.

83

Apply furring strips to outside wall, Illus. 32. Space furring strips 16" on centers. This permits applying paneling to stairwell with adhesive or nails.

If stairs require a one or two step platform, Illus. 115, 116, you can use 2 x 4, 2 x 6, 2 x 8 for a base platform. 2 x 4 on edge covered with ⅝" plywood provides a 4⅛" platform; 2 x 6 measures 6⅛"; 2 x 8 — 7⅞". When a two step platform is required, cut 2 x 4 legs to height required, Illus. 117, 97. Cut 2 x 6 or 2 x 8 frame for platform to overall size space permits. Reinforce legs with scrap pieces of 2 x 4 nailed to 2 x 8 and to leg.

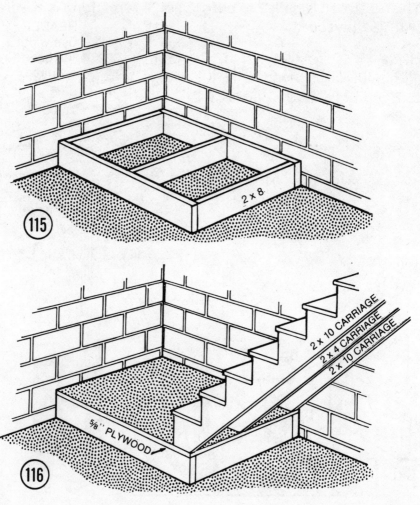

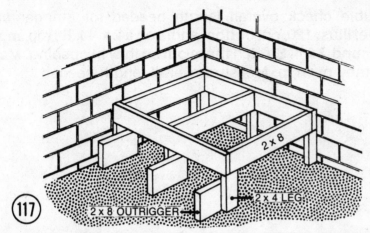

(117)

2 x 8

2 x 4 LEG

2 x 8 OUTRIGGER

The first tread is nailed to outriggers. The platform is covered with ⅝" plyscord.

Use a 1 x 12 or 5/4 x 12" for stringers; 2 x 10 carriages, Illus. 118, 119. If you need a third carriage, use a 2 x 4 and nail cutouts from 2 x 10 carriage.

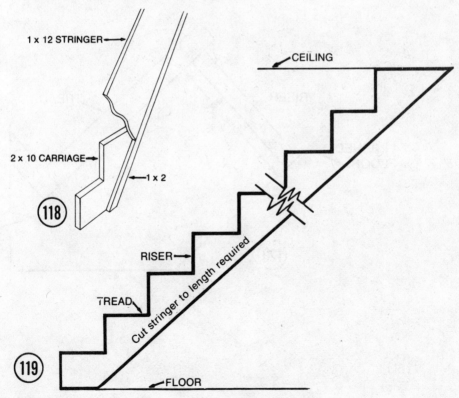

1 x 12 STRINGER

CEILING

2 x 10 CARRIAGE

1 x 2

(118)

RISER

Cut stringer to length required

TREAD

(119)

FLOOR

85

To double check overall length needed for stringer and carriage, Illus. 120, cut bottom angle on a 2 x 4 x 6', top angle on a second 2 x 4. Stretch these out so they fit opening. Mark where they overlap. Measure overall length needed.

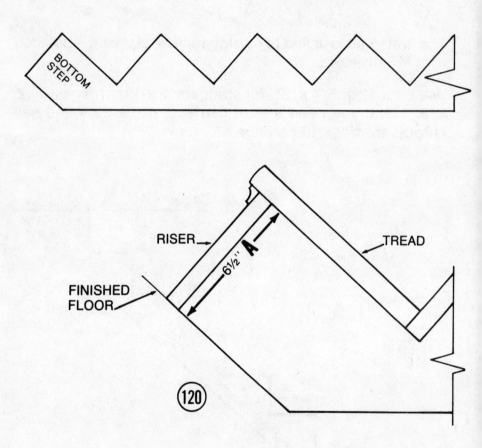

RISER

TREAD

6½" **A**

FINISHED FLOOR

(120)

Stock stair treads and risers, Illus. 120, are routed as shown. Apply glue before assembly.

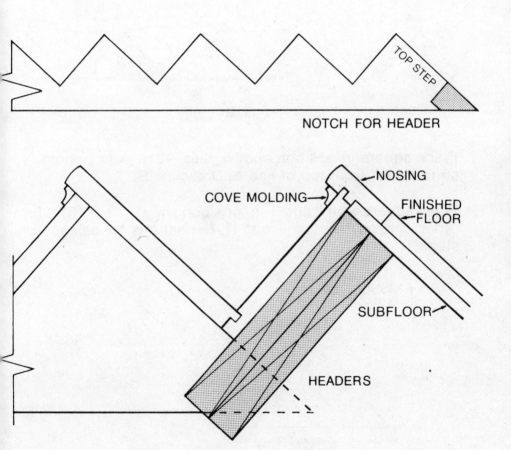

TOP STEP

NOTCH FOR HEADER

NOSING

COVE MOLDING

FINISHED FLOOR

SUBFLOOR

HEADERS

To lay out carriages having an 8" riser, 9" tread, place square in position shown for first step, Illus. 121. Draw line A.

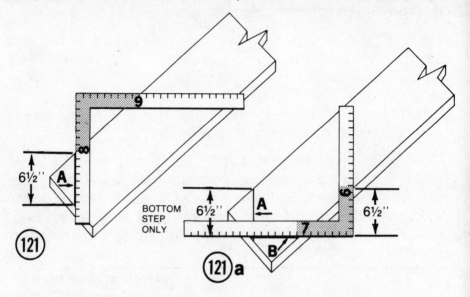

Place square in position shown, Illus. 121a, with bottom of square 6½" from top of line A. Draw line B.

Place square with 8 and 9" in position shown, Illus. 121b, for other steps. Draw line T and R. Repeat this for balance of steps.

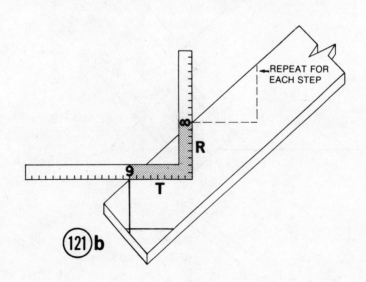

Illus. 94 shows 12 risers, 11 treads. Most millwork houses sell oak treads up to 10½'', and will cut these to width required. Buy precut treads and risers to size required.

Nail 1 x 2 to 2 x 10 carriage in position shown, Illus. 118. Nail stringer to carriage, then nail assembled stringer and carriage to header, Illus. 94. Nail cutouts from 2 x 10 carriage to 2 x 4, Illus. 116, and use this for a middle carriage. This provides more support for stairs. It also provides a nailor for gypsum board on ceiling under stairs.

Build partition to length desired, Illus. 122. Since you want to move furniture down stairs, consider how many steps you will want exposed. Spike stringer to studs. Frame in under stringer with a supporting partition, built to size required, Illus. 123. Use 2 x 4 for shoe, plate and studs. After erecting partitions, remove temporary bracing.

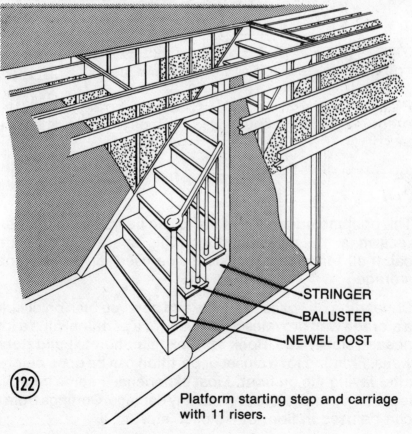

STRINGER
BALUSTER
NEWEL POST

(122)

Platform starting step and carriage with 11 risers.

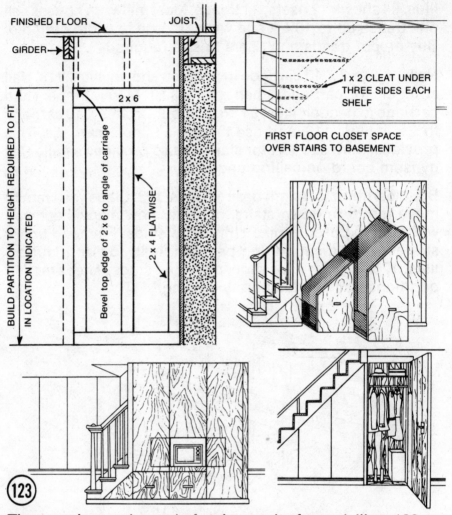

FINISHED FLOOR

JOIST

GIRDER

2 x 6

BUILD PARTITION TO HEIGHT REQUIRED TO FIT IN LOCATION INDICATED

Bevel top edge of 2 x 6 to angle of carriage

2 x 4 FLATWISE

1 x 2 CLEAT UNDER THREE SIDES EACH SHELF

FIRST FLOOR CLOSET SPACE OVER STAIRS TO BASEMENT

123

The opening under end of stairs can be framed, Illus. 123, to receive a ¾" plywood door. This space can provide a catch-all for suitcases, skis, or be used for canned goods storage.

Depending on space available and how you plan on dividing, a storage wall provides the privacy of a partition, plus a lot of needed closet area. Book #634 explains how to build storage walls. Framing for a closet or partition can be done before or after laying tile on floor. Most experienced home improvers leave this to the last to prevent any damage. Cuttings from tile can be used in floor of a closet, etc.

90

Apply glue to each riser and nail it in place with 8 penny finishing nails. Apply glue to bottom of tread where it butts against carriage, and to back edge where it butts against riser, Illus. 94.

Draw lines on each tread to indicate exact center of middle carriage. Drill holes through tread*. Nail through tread into center of carriage with 10 penny finishing nails.

Nail through riser into back edge of tread with 6 penny box nails. Retailers sell nosing that can be glued and nailed to edge of first floor flooring. They also sell a circle corner starting step, Illus. 124. Those who buy stair components should find out what's available locally, where each is used and space required prior to purchase.

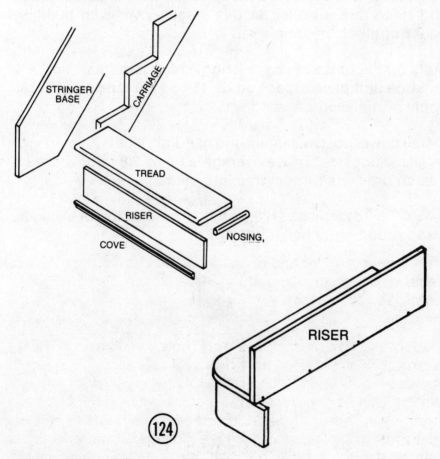

*Some treads can be nailed without drilling.

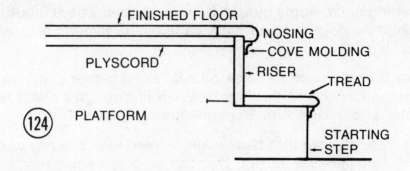

FINISHED FLOOR

NOSING

—COVE MOLDING

PLYSCORD

←RISER

TREAD

(124) PLATFORM

STARTING
←STEP

Brad cove molding below tread, Illus. 124.

We recommend nailing ¾" plyscord to carriage for temporary steps during construction, Illus. 116. If finished treads and risers are installed at this stage, cover with building paper until job is completed.

Build first floor partitions to length space requires. Use 2 x 4 for shoe and plate. Space studs 16" on centers, Illus. 111A. Apply prefinished plywood.

Install newel post, balusters and handrail, Illus. 122, at height retailer suggests. These average 2'6" to 2'8" above tread. Fasten brackets for handrail into studs.

A ½ x 2¼" base, Illus. 125, can be nailed to top of stringer, also around entry hall, Illus. 126.

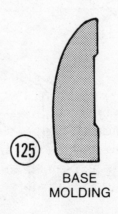

(125)

BASE
MOLDING

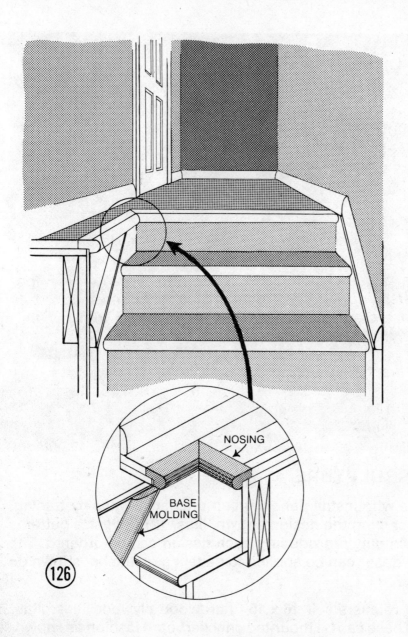

NOSING

BASE
MOLDING

126

Those installing an outside entry door should build a canopy,
Illus. 93, with or without a trellis. Complete details for
building this project are explained in Book #607 How to
Build Fences, Gates, Outdoor Projects.

(127)

PLYSCULPTURE

Those who install paneling can dramatize walls by tracing, then carving the design shown, Illus. 127. Full size patterns that simplify reproducing each design can be ordered. The same decor can be applied to paneling on the bar shown on page 7.

Many retailers sell 16 x 16" hardwood plywood tiles, Illus. 128 . These can be mounted checkerboard fashion as shown, Illus. 129. The designs can also be applied with equal success to doors and to other hardwood or hardboard panels.

When a hand held router is equipped with a depth gauge, Illus. 130, 131, no special skill is required to carve each design like a pro. Using an S-91 ball bit, Illus. 132, follow the traced outline.

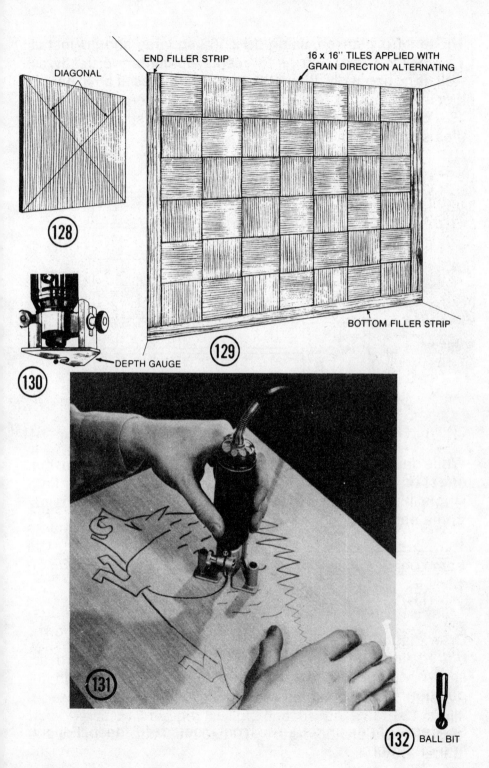

DIAGONAL

(128)

END FILLER STRIP

16 x 16'' TILES APPLIED WITH
GRAIN DIRECTION ALTERNATING

BOTTOM FILLER STRIP

(129)

DEPTH GAUGE

(130)

(131)

(132) BALL BIT

Those who plan on using 16 x 16" squares should install 1 x 2 or 1 x 3 furring strips 16", center-to-center, vertically, as well as horizontally, Illus. 133. Six 16" squares fit an 8' panel. If ceiling height is lower, or length of wall doesn't divide by 16", consider using a bottom and end filler strip, or cutting tiles slightly smaller.

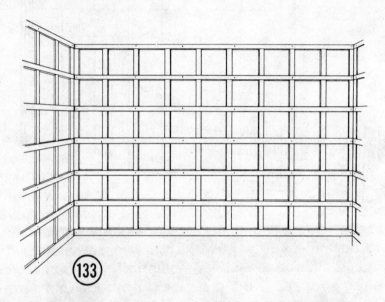

While dark grained plywood helps accentuate the design, the effect on light grains is equally interesting. Those mounting single 16 x 16" tiles should bevel edge, Illus. 134. This helps frame each design.

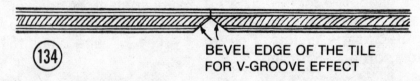

BEVEL EDGE OF THE TILE
FOR V-GROOVE EFFECT

Draw diagonal lines lightly across each panel, Illus. 128. The dotted lines on pattern cross at center. Align pattern as shown, Illus. 135. Using carbon paper, trace design in position.

Set depth gauge on router so it only routs 1/16" deep. Follow line of pattern.

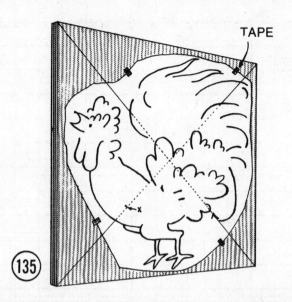

TAPE

(135)

Those working on natural (no-wax) mahogany, walnut or darker plywood should apply a thin coat of orange shellac. Thin shellac with an equal part of alcohol. Allow to dry. After routing design, paint with white water base paint. Before paint has a chance to set, wipe paint off non-routed areas with a rag wrapped around a block of wood. This permits paint in routed area to remain. Carefully remove all paint from surface. Allow paint to dry thoroughly then rub unpainted surface with fine steel wool or #00 sandpaper wrapped around a square block of wood. Wipe away all dust.

Mount squares to furring strips with contact cement or adhesive tile retailer recommends. Allow cement to set time manufacturer specifies. If necessary, use ¾" wire brads to fasten corners to furring.

The Plysculpture pattern shown, Illus. 127, is #705 Tile-A-Wall. A wide selection of other Easi-Bild full size Plysculpture patterns are available. No special skill or artistic talent is required to transform plywood or hardboard wall paneling into decorative murals. These patterns simplify decorating folding floor screens, flush panel and kitchen cabinet doors.

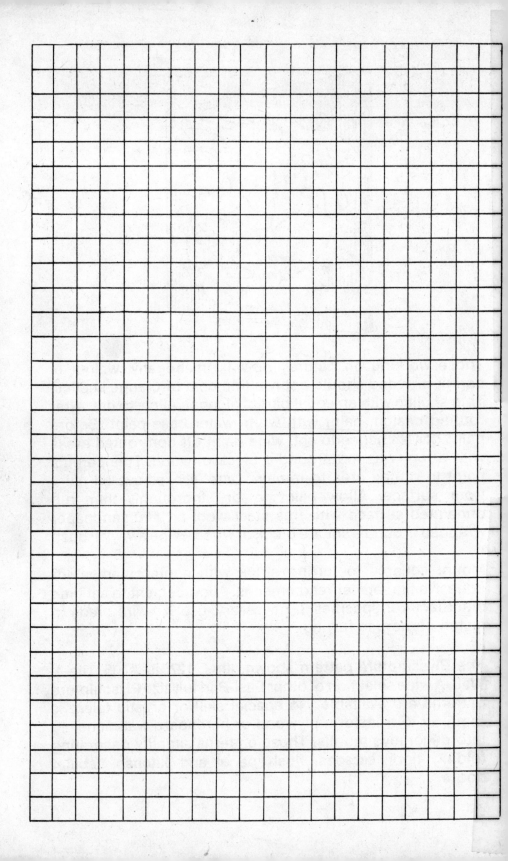